SUSTAINABLE DEVELOPMNT AND PRINCIPLES OF SOCIAL SYSTEMS MODELING

Dr. Alexander Makarenko

Title: SUSTAINABLE DEVELOPMNT AND PRINCIPLES OF SOCIAL SYSTEMS MODELING

Author: Dr. Alexander Makarenko

ISBN: 978-1-63902-004-1

Cover image: www.pixabay.com

Publisher: Generis Publishing
Online orders: www.generis-publishing.com
Contact email: info@generis-publishing.com

ANNOTATION

This book proposes one of the possible approaches to solving problems of modeling large social systems. First, the issues that needs to be considered when developing models are qualitatively described. In this regard, analogies of the behavior of large social systems with artificial neural networks are indicated. Some issues of the mental properties of an individual are given, which should be taken into account when building models. One of the main among them is taking into account the internal image of the external world in the representation of the individual. Consideration of the inner image allowed proposing new ways to consider other common problems - for example, the archetypes in consciousness.

Consideration of the issues indicated above made it possible to propose appropriate mathematical models that allowed, for example, describing some aspects of the problem of sustainable development. Some issues of anticipation in to public systems are considered.

The book also contains mathematical models of both large social systems and some mental processes of individuals. In some cases, illustrations of the application of the proposed models are given: to geopolitics, the stock market, the formation of public opinion.

Special attention is also paid to discussing the formation of knowledge and their role as the main resource of the process of sustainable development of society.

PREFACE

In the modern picture of the world, the idea of a person and his interaction with the environment are of great importance. One striking example is the concept of sustainable development. Economic processes are another example. All this (and much more) poses as one of the most important tasks the mathematical modeling of various personal aspects of both an individual and large groups of people, for example, society as a whole.

Research on such problems is rapidly developing, but it is still a long way to fully solve such problems, especially in connection with the problem of modeling the subject / object interaction.

This book proposes one of the possible approaches to solving such problems. First, the issues that should to be considered when developing models are qualitatively described. In this regard, analogies of the behavior of large social systems with artificial ones are indicated, some issues of the mental properties of an individual are given, which should be taken into account when building models. One of the main among them is taking into account the internal image of the external world in the representation of the individual. Consideration of the inner image allowed us to propose new ways to consider other common problems - for example, the archetypes of consciousness.

Consideration of the issues indicated above made it possible to propose appropriate mathematical models that allowed, for example, describing some aspects of the problem of sustainable development. In particular, we managed to consider some issues of anticipation in relation to public systems.

Along the way, the book contains mathematical models of both large social systems and some mental processes of individuals. In some cases, illustrations of the application of the proposed models are given: to geopolitics, the stock market, the formation of public opinion.

Special attention is also paid to discussing the formation of knowledge and their role as the main resource of the process of sustainable development of society.

The book is composed in such a way that the sections of the book are as independent from each other as possible.

The author of the book expresses deep gratitude to S. Levkov, V. Solia, V. Zelenskiy, S. Laskavenko, Z. Klestova, E. Samorodov and many others for cooperation in one form or another.

TABLE OF CONTENTS

4

PART 1

QUALITATIVE CONSIDEREATIONS OF SUSTAINABLE DEVELOPMENT AND SOCIETY PROPERTIES

CHAPTER I

SYSTEM ANALYSIS, FORMAL DEFINITION AND MODELS FOR SUSTAINABLE DEVELOPMENT

1. Introduction

The concept of sustainable development (SD) in relatively short period of time gained sufficient popularity and became a real aspect policymakers pay attention to as well as became the subject of numerous publications (Rogers 2007 [30]; Sheffran et al. 2012 [31]; Daly 2014 [7]; Dasgupta 2007 [8]; Theory 2013 [35]; De Tombe 2015 [9]; Brundtland Commission 1987 [5]; Weizsacker, Wijkman [39]; Zgurovsky and Statyukha 2010 [40]). Perhaps the basic definition is known somewhere since the beginning of the 90s. However, there are many modifications to the interpretation of this definition, and they depend most likely on the scientific interests of researchers considering the problems of sustainable development, further to reduce SD. It should be noted that, as a rule, these are verbal or qualitative definitions of SD, or at best the study of individual process systems, or SD indices. Recall that when considering SD as a basic definition, the definition (1987) of the Brundtland Commission (Brundtland Commision 1987 [5]; Our Common Future 2017 [25]) is adopted: "Sustainable development is development that meets the needs of the present without compromising the ability of future generations to meet their own needs". However, after 25 years it becomes necessary to further develop both the foundations of the concept and those that allow formalization and use in modeling processes. Recently new 17 general goals for development of society for 2015–2030 years have been proposed by UN (Goals 2015 [12]; Weizsacker, Wijkman 2018 [39]). But one of the obstacles for implementation of SD concept is the small number of applications of strict approaches from operation research and mathematical modeling to problem. However, a number of analytical studies on SD discuss these questions (for examples (Chichilnisky 1996 [6]; Bergh and Nijkampf 1991 [4]; Aubin and Saint-Pierre 2006 [1]; Scheffran and Pickl 2000 [32]; Rand and Wilson 1993 [29]; Pezzey 1997 [27]; Paksoy et al. 2011 [26]; Theory 2013 [35]; Hellman et al. 2017 [14]) and a source of further references see Weizsacker, Wijkman 2018 [39]).

But usually such investigations concern particular problems or aspects of SD. Further formalization of the concept and models largely depends on the scope of applications and at the same time can also vary greatly depending on the models used, therefore, it continues to be very relevant. Thus further development of methods and models should be considered. Therefore, in this paper we try to highlight some aspects related to SD. At first we propose system analysis of SD problem. The role of obstacles in SD is reconsidered and illustrations of this are described. Then the new formal definition of sustainable development problem is proposed. Afterwards we introduce the class of models that allow to consider many SD problems. Also the propositions on new indices for sustainability are developed. Finally the role of anticipation and education in SD is discussed.

2. Considerations to development of the formalization of the concept of SD

In this Section we discuss some aspects that should be clarified before discussing the formalization of SD i.e. modeling. We follow an inductive way, moving from simpler and clearer tasks to more complex ones, so as to result in some understanding of aspects relating to the most common socio-naturaleconomic-technical-political systems SNET-integral complexes. The presentation in this part is carried out at illustrative level.

2.1 Three aspects of complex SNET

Society begins to pay more attention to SD, so ideas SD concept now appears in many administrative projects on management – systems management – environmental, urban, cultural, economic, etc. In general, the idea of sustainability and sustainable development has about tens of millions of links in search engines (for example, in GOOGLE). Often, in this case, first of all, the idea of conserving resources and somewhere in an implicit form is considered, nevertheless, the second part of the definition of the Brundtland Commission on solving the problems of future generations, that is, for many ordinary managers sustainability is considered for a short time interval of a maximum of 10–15 years (in fact this part coincides with the practice of planning management links). Secondly, considering problems related to SD, it is clear that a large role is played both by the spatial scales of systems (land → continents → regions → countries → territories of countries → cities and individual landscapes → subsystem elements, and temporal scales, for example, from times of the orders of geological epochs to the periods of changes in landscapes and climate changes, to annual intervals (and less, if necessary). There are also clearly traced different timelines in other aspects of SNET: for example – civilizations → styling → cyclical phenomena in cultural areas processes → annual scales →, etc. Many scales are associated with economic and industrial activity: Cameron ($\approx$ 200 years), Schumpeter and Kondratiev ($\approx$ 50 years), cycles in construction ($\approx$ 10-12 years), in agro-industry ($\approx$ 1 year), etc. It is also worth recalling the scale associated with biology: the time of change in the genotype and phenotype, the laws of natural selection (for example, as in Darwin's theory of evolution), the generation change in human communities.

2.2 Geometrical illustrations to SD problems

Starting from the first works by J. Forrester (J. Forrester 1971), who laid the foundations of the SD problem, the presentation of the results of calculations and the presentation of concepts in the form of graphic diagrams played an important role. When such schedules are considered, a dependence of some magnitude (for example, the amount of population or oil reserves, or pollution) is usually given, etc. of the time, or the dependence of all values is given on the same graph. However, the very concept of SD, at least those aspects related to the depletion of resources for the next generations, is obscured (the graphs shown in Fig. 1 are typical).

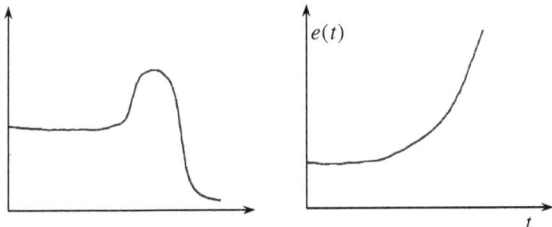

Dependency of population (left) and pollution of nature (right) (following J. Forrester)

However, graphs of this kind represent only one aspect of SNET, while illustrations should be considered in the multidimensional space of all components. Given these considerations, a one-dimensional illustration of SD should look slightly different, for example, the evolution of the parameter $p(t)$

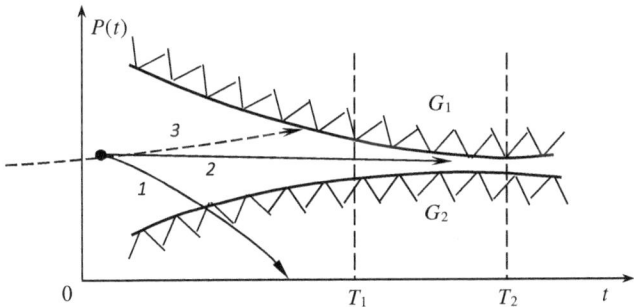

Fig. 2. Various scenarios for the evolution of the system

11

under the condition of limited resources G1 and G2 in Fig. 2 means the restrictions that limit possible trajectories in the system.

The values T1 and T2 on Fig. 2 conditionally show the boundaries of generations that succeed each other. Then in the situation of Fig. 2, the trajectory 1 corresponds to the strict case of unsupported development, when the resources are not enough for this generation, and the trajectory 2 – to the case when sustainability is just provided, then how SD is most often treated in practical management of territories, systems, organizations corresponds to trajectory 3, i.e. planning within the same generation. However, Fig. 2 is very simplistic. Let us give further complications at the same level. Usually, natural resources are still exhausted, so the situation in Fig. 2 should rather look like Fig. 3.

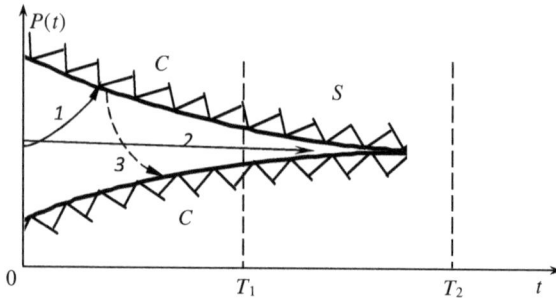

Fig. 3. Exhaustion of development resources

Domain S corresponds to the impossibility of functioning of systems after

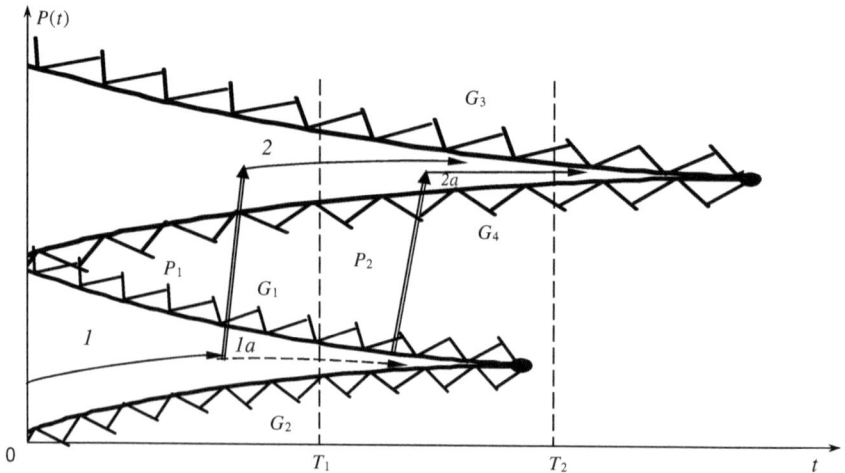

Fig. 4. Transition from one resource base (with borders $G_1 - G_2$) to another (with borders $G_3 - G_4$)

12

exhausted resources. Note that the trajectory 2 is possible with the best fixed control method. Note that in these illustrations we assume that the SNET trajectory can not overcome the constraints and the crisis (at point C), with change the trajectory (1) Fig. 1 Dependency of population (left) and pollution of nature (right) (following J. Forrester) Fig. 2 Various scenarios for the evolution of the system Fig. 3 Exhaustion of development resources or the catastrophe (at point G) without the continuing the trajectory occurs. For example, if the restriction is the oil

reserves for transport, operating only on gasoline. In fact, of course, the history of SNET teaches that evolution with time is not so unambiguously pessimistic, and because of the need for systems, there are changes that can allow the system to exist and develop further. This is illustrated in Fig. 4.

This means that in some way the system can move from one type to another. For example, from oil and coal to nuclear power. Let P1 and P2 correspond to possible paths of the transition, we discuss below. Note that an inverse transition, for example, from path 2 to 1 (or from 2a to 1) is also possible. This can, in the case of the energy, mean the loss of nuclear technology (either because of disasters, or because of the loss of knowledge about technology). Note also that the constraints on the figures depend on the time (and in fact, on the other parameters). With the illustrative manner of Fig. 1–4 the restrictions are in fact a projection of multidimensional constraints for the SNET trajectory. In turn, the restrictions in a sense are dual to trajectories – they can be found as the boundaries of possible trajectories. By the way, the type of constraints for one- and two-dimensional figures 1–4 can be obtained both in the theory of catastrophes or in the features of differentiable mappings (in those cases when they are applicable) as projections of multidimensional surfaces onto a plane. In fact, hypothetical transitions P1, P2, in Fig. 4 should occur in additional ('hidden') for this type of 'onedimensional' measurement patterns. Also Fig. 1–4 reveals some of the system characterizing indices. So, if only the growth of the parameter $P(t)$ was important in Fig. 3, the value of $P(T)$ would be the index of progress ('development'). However, it is clear that it alone (without taking into account the limitations) can not characterize the sustainability of the trajectory and the index of sustainable development must be built in a special way. Fig. 4 Transition from one resource base (with borders G1–G2) to another (with borders G3–G4) Many options for setting up problems about SD can be seen.

Example 2.1 (economy). G. Chickilinisky (Chichilinsky 1996 [6]) in his work on mathematical research primarily economic problems formulated specifically for the economy criteria SD (even in the form of axioms, which, unlike others, take into account aspects of balanced consideration of the interests of the generation (and not to the detriment of each other). They considerably differ from the results obtained from the condition of obtaining maximum profit. There are also some ideas of R. Solow and partly (although ideologically broader, E. Nelson and C. Dosi) to the same direction.

Example 2.2 (evolutionary biology). Another class of works that is useful for thinking over the idea of SD, is centered around models of evolution in biology with a change in the genotype and the study of the stability of communities (populations). Among the works on this topic one should note the work of D. Rand with co-authors (Rand and Wilson 1993 [29]). These studies are concentrated in fact on the study of the attractors of the corresponding systems, their properties and stability under the influence of a change in the composition of the system. However, in these works only problems related to biology are considered.

Example 2.3. Self-organized criticality and transformational transitions. P. Bak, R. Sneppen consider problems of the transition of complex systems to an unstable state and avalanche unloading processes from such states. In addition, rapid transitions between almost equilibrium states – the so-called punctuated transitions (Bak and Sneppen 1993 [2]) – were studied. However, the observed regularities, although they give some understanding of the effects in such systems, only matter as part of the overall picture. These examples differ from the enormous variety of other works on SD (especially descriptive or even philosophical plan) by the availability of mathematical models and their research. However, they do not give an idea for formalization the general SD scheme (although they often provide leading considerations for particular problems and allow us to formulate ideas about formalization SD description). Therefore, in the next section, we will try to give some primary considerations for the formalization of SD.

3. Formalization of the description sustainability and sustainability development

The reasoning is carried out for two cases of a simpler local and global in some sense introduced below: first, we consider what we call a local scheme (with only one generation examined) that solves only its local time problems, proceeding again from local criteria. At second, we indicate the structures and concepts that should be taken into account in the problem of local SD.

3.1 Formalization of SD process description

In order to formalize the SD description first of all it is necessary to represent the elements of the systems, processes and criteria which should be accounted. After the analysis of many existing investigations (including references in given paper) we can propose the list of 12 issues which should be used for general description of SD. In this subsection we will not consider in detail the properties of these (and the following description elements), but only try to identify which structures should be considered. For example, without special need, we will not consider possible metric and topological structures, order relations, symmetries, etc. The elements of description are:

1. Parameters of the system and their description (external, internal, control, etc.) we denote as the set of parameters {Par}.

2. Equations describing the systems {Equat}.

3. The set of trajectories of the systems {Traj}.

4. Limitations on the trajectories and parameters of the system-the set {Ω} and set of boundary points (boundaries) of constraints {$\partial\Omega$}.

5. A set of sustainability criteria (SCrit) or SD criteria {SD Crit}.

6. The set of external control parameters {Contr}.

7. A set representing the age structure of populations on the interval [0, T] {Age}. If there is no explicit interval, we will write {Age}.

8. The set of initial conditions {Init}.

9. The structures of the system {StSys}, of the processes {StProc} and of individuals {StInd}.

10. Additional requirements for components (desirable) – additional to mandatory restrictions {Ω} and {$\partial\Omega$}. We denote them by {Aux}.

11. Descriptions of the decision-making process {Decis}.

12. A set of uncertainties in the system {NonDef}. Now we describe what is the SD problem.

Definition of SD problem.

To find objects (the complex of system, processes, individual's properties, control parameters and decision-making) from {St = {StSys} { R StProc} { R StInd}}, {Contr}, {Decis}, such that for such object we obtain a trajectory for the evolution of the system tr {Traj} that (t) belong {SDCrit} { R Aux}, where (t) means computed value of the SD criterion at time t on the trajectory tr, and the results of the calculation must belong to {SDCrit} and {Aux} at any time.

(The symbol R indicates the belonging of the parameters to all specified sets of (different) parameters). The meaning of the definition is demonstrated on simple illustrations in the form of geometric pictures for better understanding. Here we pose some comments to the definition above.

Remark 1. To the 12 structures mentioned above, we can add one more – the set of models {Models}, if we use modeling.

Remark 2. The sets {StSys}, {StProc} and {StInd} of the list item 9 can be used if indeed such objects are arranged. But one can confidently assume that such structures really exist (even if nothing is known about them explicitly).

Remark 3. When considering different systems, one can use the categorical approach in this formulation and try to distinguish the category of systems with the sustainable development of CatSD.

Remark 4. Considering the possible multi-valued trajectories of the system (which can appear in case, particulary, SNET includes the social component), so instead of one trajectory tr one can use the formulations with the trajectory funnel Ptr.

Remark 5. The existence of fluctuations and other uncertainties is also possible (by the way, this is important in assessing the risks). Then one can take into account the uncertainty in the objects, considering some sets of 1–12 supplemented with a description of the uncertainties. Bearing in mind the structure of Definition for the SD problem, one can move on and expand and at the same time refine the definition.

Remark 6. Considering the presence of many different generations (for simplicity, we are talking about two generations below). For example, it can be that two generations have different SD criteria, then {SDCrit} = {SDCrit} (Generation 1) { R SDCritGeneration 2}. There can be different for the generations control restrictions {RCtrl} = {RCtrl} (Generation 1) { R RCtrl} (Generation 2). In principle, it can be that {SDCrit} = {SDCrit} (Generation 1) { R MSDCrit} (Generation 2), where {MSDCrit} (Generation 2) is the set of possible criteria, SD of the second generation. We can not know exactly {MSDCrit} (Generation 2) because it depends on future technologies, but in fact on future knowledge {Knowl} (Generation 2) about which we can only speculate (we believe that a lot of current knowledge of the given generation

16

{Knowl} (Generation 1) is known in the first approximation – or, for example, it is the set of knowledge realized in technologies).

Description of SD problem, given above, can be useful in application of operational research and mathematical modeling. In application OR and mathematical modeling for concrete SD problems such flowchart processes can take place. At first the system analysis gives the structure of problem, systems and elements. Then mathematical models and mathematical formulation for criteria are chosen. After this proposed definition of SD can be applied. Of course it can be very difficult task, especially for global SD problem. Just formalizing the SD problem for smaller systems usually is difficult and strongly depends on considered system. So, below we give only some examples for illustration of aspect of proposed definition. Example 3.1. We can define the set {SDCrit} as a set, where some indices satisfy the accepted by experts representations about SD. That is in this case the set of indices {Ind}, which corresponds to expert opinion about the SD-set {IndSD}. Then the process will be with SD if ind { R Ind}, and ind { R IndSD}. In this case, of course, many subtle details of processes and system behavior are not taken into account. We note incidentally some interesting papers containing the search for SD indices (see the literature in Rogers 2007 [30]; Theory 2013 [35]; Weizsacker, Wijkman 2018 [39]; Zgurovsky and Statyukha 2010 [40]). By the way, in J. Forrester's works, knowledge does not enter explicitly into the composition of the main variables.

Example 3.2. (Works by G. Chickilnisky (Chickilnisky 1996 [6])). In them, as far as one can be judge, indices are formed only for economic reasons.

Example 3.3. (The work of D. Rand and H. Wilson (Rand and Wilson [29])). {St} in them varies with time, and {SDCrit} can be formulated mathematically strictly.

Example 3.4. It is not excluded that {SDCrit} can be formed using the Lyapunov function.

Example 3.5. Evolutionary economy. It is possible, in principle, to compile a comparison table for SD studies in this formalization

Example 3.6. (Local SD). A simpler case, if the situation does not change significantly, simple models (as a rule, they correspond to one of the "pillars") system and without taking into account the generation change. It is clear that the SD criteria can be written taking into account various factors (for example, the speed along the trajectory, the energy reserve for control, etc.). In this form it resembles the tasks of motion control with mathematical statements (motion control with constraint). The proposed scheme of consideration seems suit any variant of SD processes, both descriptive (verbal) and specific practical problems or for tasks already having formalization in the form of mathematical problems. The review and comparison of mathematical productions would be very useful.

3.2 The role of strong and weak anticipation in SD processes

We point out here some important problems of using the SD concept and considering the local and global aspects of SD. A useful tool in the practice of regional management is the use of mathematical modeling to predict the flow of processes in various fields: ecology, economics, social. Mathematical modeling in regional planning is used to predict possible scenarios for the evolution of real natural, technical, and social systems. Typically, real regional management experts view SD as a certain 'best' mode in the operation of a particular system. Consideration of the 'needs of the next generations' is often neglected. Also, usually with local management, they do not consider the means and tasks for modeling the distant future. Note that a 'long-term' prediction is most often impossible primarily due to the initial complexity of such systems. Secondly, the impossibility of forecasting a single path of development for large technical-economic-ecological systems is recognized by all. Up now, the arguments about the "further needs of the generations" are applicable rather when considering global theoretical problems. But SD processes can be treated adequately from the point of view of systems by anticipation, especially with the "strong" and "weak" anticipation introduced by Daniel Dubois since the 1990s (Dubois 2001 [10]; Makarenko 2002 [18]; Makarenko 2013 [19]). Many formal definitions have been described in the literature (see for example (Makarenko 2013 [19]; Dubois 2001 [10]). Here we recall one of the definitions that is useful for understanding the role of anticipation in SD. D. Dubois shared a weak anticipation, that is, when systems use the model of themselves and the environment to calculate future states, and strong anticipation, that is, when the system uses itself to create its future states. In the latter case, the anticipation is no longer similar to the prediction" (Dubois 2001 [10], [11]). Therefore, 'local management' SD (using prediction) corresponds to a weak anticipation. But the situation with the global SD problem is completely different. Only the formal definition of SD above (subsection 3.1) makes it possible to use the strong anticipation property for the global systems under consideration. That is, it is allowed to consider the future behavior of large social systems in the case of impossibility of prediction. Some possible confirmation of the anticipation property for social systems has been described earlier.

Also, many applications of such ideas (anticipation) for SD problems can be used for real system research and in management practice. Here we only need to emphasize the importance of SD education and the scientific system as one of the main tasks for SD of any large social system. For example, the possibility of sustainable development of the energy industry and the development of energy resources depends strongly on the development, first of all, of new knowledge about physical processes. For example, the development of nuclear power plants depends strongly on the development of nuclear physics. Thus, the ideas described in this subsection support the possibilities for further development of the formal definition of SD and allow us to formulate the SD problems on a rigorous basis. In the following subsections we will consider several problems of such kind.

3.3 Anticipation and possible consequences in models

We recall very briefly the descriptions of the anticipation (Dubois 2001 [10]; Makarenko 2002 [18], 2013 [19]). A weak anticipation means that the system has a model for predicting future behavior. Strong anticipation means that the future state of the system is not known, but is taken into account to assess the transition at a given time. The first essential new property in this case in the behavior of model solutions is the possibility of a multivalued solution (this set of possible values of the solution for certain instants of time exist under the unique initial conditions of the system (Makarenko 2002 [18], 2013 [19])). This can be interpreted as the possibility of many development scenarios for real social systems. The second key property is connected with the fact that the real social system has a single realization of the historical path (the trajectory of the system actually being realized). That is, the social system as a whole makes a choice of its own trajectory at any time. The local SD process is usually a process with a weak anticipation. Global SD processes are strongly anticipative. Consideration of scenarios and selection of a solution (scenario) can be considered on the basis of consideration of multivalued solutions and the choice of a single trajectory (Makarenko and Klestova 1999 [21]; Makarenko 1997 [22], 1998 [23]; Beradze et al. 1999 [3], Levkov et al. 1998 [17]). In what follows some geometrical illustrations of possible situations are presented.

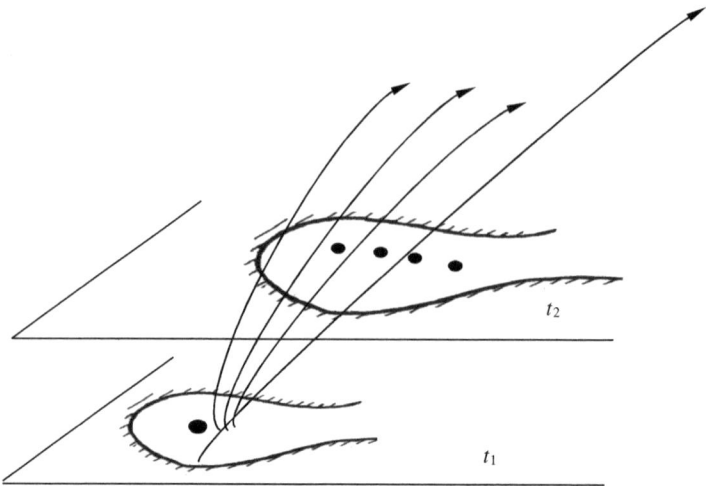

Fig. 5. Multiplicity of possible scenarios in a system with strong anticipation

Fig. 5 illustrates the evolution of a system with a strong anticipation with time-limited resource constraints. New in comparison with conventional models is the case of the possibility of the existence of alternative scenarios. Fig. 6

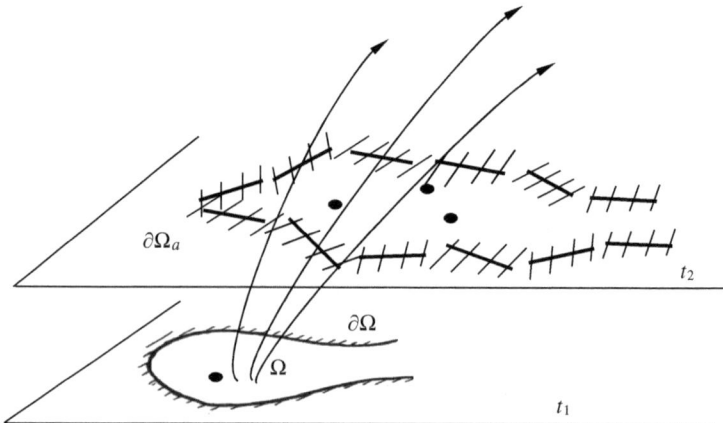

Fig. 6. Unknown virtual anticipated restrictions in a system with strong anticipation

corresponds to a much more complex (but also closer to reality) situation, where the limitations in the future change with time and depend on the possible evolution of the system. Moreover, in this case, the constraints themselves can acquire a many-valued form, which significantly complicates the mathematical formulation of the corresponding problems. Such a picture in principle just corresponds best to the situation of unknown future knowledge.

We note that the restrictions in this case can be formalized as a mathematical object in various ways – as nonlinear equations, in classes of fuzzy sets or statistical distributions; other types of uncertainties; differential equations; variational inequalities, etc. Further, when considering constraints unknown in time, other aspects should also be considered (for example, geometric or topological, see Fig. 4). Note that the above considerations are also new when considering and assessing risks in large socio-technical and economic systems.

REFERENCES

1. Aubin J.-P., Saint-Pierre P. An Introduction to Viability Theory and Management of Renewable Resourses. In: Decision-making and Risk Management in Sustainability Science, (eds. T. Kropp and J. Scheffran). N.Y.: Nova Science Publisher (2006)
2. Bak P., Sneppen K. Punctured Equilibrium and Criticality in a Simple model of evolution, Phys.Rev.Lett, 71, No. 24, P. 4083–4089 (1993)
3. Beradze M., Mnatsakanyan M., Makarenko A., Chikriy A. Optimal control in geopolitical problems, Vestn. Kharkiv Polytechnic Institute, No. 72, P. 8–12 (1999)
4. Van den Bergh J.C., Nijkamp P. Operationalizing Sustainable Development: Dynamic Economic Models, Ecological Economic, Vol. 4, P. 11–34 (1991)
5. Brundtland Commission. Report on the World Commission on Environment and Development. United Nations General Assembly, 96th Plenary Meeting 11 Dec. 1987. A/RES/42/187 (1987)
6. Chichilnisky G. An axiomatic approach to sustainable development, Social Chois and Welfare, Vol. 2, Issue 3, P. 231–257 (1996)
7. Daly H. From Uneconomic Growth to a Steady State Economy, Advanced in Ecological Economics, Chetlenham, UK (2014)
8. Dasgupta P. The idea of sustainable Development, Sustainability Science, Vol. 2, P. 5–11 (2007)
9. De Tombe D. Handling Societal Complexity. Springer-Verlag, Berlin-Heidelberg (2015)
10. Dubois D. Incursive and hyperincursive systems, fractal machine and anticipatory logic. Computing Anticipatory Systems: CASYS 2000 – Fourth International Conference. Published by the American Institute of Physics, AIP Conference Proceedings. 573, P. 437–451 (2001)
11. Dubois D. Theory of incursive synchronization and application to the anticipation of the chaotic epidemic, Int. J. of Comput Anticip. Syst. (Liege) , Vol. 10", P. 3–18 (2001)
12. Goals, Sustainable development goals, https://sustainabledevelopment.un.org/?menu=1300 (2015)
13. Haykin S. Neural Networks: Comprehensive Foundations, MacMillan: N.Y. (1994)
14. Hellman F., Shultz P., Grabow C., Heitzig J., Kunsths J. Survivability of Deterministic Dynamic Systems, Scientific Reports (Nature), Vol. 6: 29654 (2016)

15. Kapitsa S., Kurdyumov S., Malinetskiy G. Synergetics and forecasts of the future, Moscow, Nauka (1997)
16. Lefebvre V.A. Algebra of conscience. Dordrecht: Reidell (1982)
17. Levkov S., Makarenko A., Zelinsky V. Neuronet type models for stock market trading patterns, Proc. 5th Ukrainian Conference AUTOMATICA'98, Kiev, May, 1998, P. 162–166 (1998)
18. Makarenko A. Anticipating in the modeling of large social systems – neuronets with internal structure and multivaluedness, Int. J. of Computing Anticipatory Systems, 13, P. 77–92 (2002)
19. Makarenko A. Neuronet models of global processes with intellectual elements, International business: Innovation, Psychology, Economics, 4, No. 1(6), P. 65–83 (2013)
20. Makarenko A. About models of global socio-economic processes, Reports of the Ukrainian Academy of Sciences, No. 12, P. 85–87 (1994) [in Russian]
21. Makarenko A., Klestova Z. A new class of global models of associative memory type as a tool for considering global environmental change, Environmental Change, Adaptation, and Security, Ed. By S.C. Lonergan, NATO ASI Series, 2. Environment, Vol. 65, Kluwer Academic Publishers (1999)
22. Makarenko A. Global social conflicts and their models In: Confliktologikal expertaie: Theory and methodology. Vol. 1. Kiev: Conlictologis Association of Ukraine, P. 87–95 (1997) [in Russian]
23. Makarenko A. New Neuronet Models of Global Socio-Economical Processes // Gaming / Simulation for Policy Development and Organizational Change. J. Geurts, C. Joldersma, E. Roelofs eds, Tillburg: Tillburg University Press, P. 128–132 (1998)
24. Makarenko A. Multivaluedness Aspects in Self-Organization, Complexity and Computations Investigations by Strong Anticipation. Chapter in Book: Recent Advances in Nonlinear Dynamics and Synchronization. Eds. K. Kyamakya , W. Mathis, R. Stoop, J. Chedjou, Z. Li, Springer; Cham, P. 33–54 (2018)
25. Our Common Future, https://www.iisd.org/topic/sustainable-development (2018)
26. Paksoy T., Ozceylan E., Weber G.-W. A multi Objective Model for Optimization of a Green Supply Chain Network, Global Journal of Technology and Optimization, Vol. 2, P. 84–96 (2011)
27. Pezzey J. Sustainability constraints versus Intertemporal Concern, and Axioms Versus Data, Land Economics, Vol. 73, P. 448–466 (1997)

28. Prigogine I. The Networked Society, J. World-Syst. Res, 6, No. 3, P. 892–898 (2000)
29. Rand D.A., Wilson H.B. Evolutionary Catastrophes, Punctuated Equilibria and Gradualism in Ecosystem Evolution, Proc. Roy. Society London, Vol. 253, P. 131–141 (1993)
30. Rogers P., Jalal K.F., Boyd J.A. An Introduction to Sustainable Development, Routledge (2007)
31. Sheffran J., Brzoska M., Brauch H.-G., Link P., Schelling J. Climate Change, human Security and Violent conflict: Challenges for Societal Stability, Springer Science and Business Media, Vol. 8 (2012)
32. Scheffran J., Pickl S. Control and Game-theoretic Assessment of Climat-change: Options for Joint Implementations, Annals of Operational Research, Vol. 97, P. 203–212 (2000)
33. Soros G. Open society: reforming global capitalism, NY: Public Affairs (2000)
34. Sutton J.P., Beis J.S., Trainor L.E.H. Hierarchical model of memory and memory loss, Jour. of Phys. A: Math. Gen., 21, P. 4443–4454 (1988)
35. Theory and Implementation of Economic Models for Sustainability, Eds. J.C. van den Bergh, M.W. Hofkes, Springer (2013)
36. Vorobiev Yu.L., Malinetskiy G.G., Makhutov N.A. Theory of risk and security technology. Approach from positions of nonlinear dynamics, Proc. SICPRO'1998, Moscow: IPU, 2 p. (1998)
37. Wallerstein I. The Heritage of Sociology, The Promise of Social Science, Presidential Address, XIV-th World Congress of Sociology, Montreal, July 26, 1998, Part 2, http://fbc.binghampton.edu/iwprad2.htm (1998)
38. Watts D.J., Strogatz S. Collective dynamics of "small-world" networks, Nature, 393, P. 440–442 (1998)
39. Weizsacker E.U., Wijkman A. Come On! Capitalism, Short-termism, population and the Destruction of the Planet. N.Y.: Springer Science + Business Media, LLC (2018)
40. Zgurovsky M.Z., Statyukha G.A. Fundamentals of sustainable development of society, Part 1, Kiev: NTUU "KPI" (2010)

CHAPTER II

THE MODELS OF SOCIETY WITH ANTICIPATORY PROPERTY AND SCENARIOS APPROACH IN DECISION-MAKING

1. Introduction

Physics of the XX century has developed many tools, methods, and principles for the study of inanimate nature. This is the visible basis of modern physics. But parallel to this visible flow, there were always hidden tendencies in physics, which were associated with the desire to understand the place of man and his structure in terms of physics. It should be noted that many prominent physicists thought about such problems. For example, N. Bohr, E. Schrodinger, Y. Jordan, D. Bohm, W. Paulie, J. Wheeler. Another way to solve such problems is to study brain processes and artificial intelligence (N. Wiener, A. Rosenbluth, W. McCulloch, W. Pitts, D. Hopfield, A. Lyapunov). Recently, the problems of the observer (observer) on the micro and macro levels in quantum and classical physics have been intensively studied in classical and non-classical quantum mechanics (H. Everett, A. Shimoni, W. Shemp, P. Marser, Ch. Atmanspater, Ch. Farr).

But with the development of modern society (let us call it globalization), especially in connection with the development of informatization, understanding the functioning of society becomes more and more important. Society as a whole complex social and economic object consists of a large number of subsystems and subprocesses. Modern natural science, especially physics, has always tried to create some models and gave some understanding of such interesting objects. Naturally, one of the subsystems that were investigated by physical methods was economic. Perhaps, one of the leading methodologies in the physical application to economics is the theory of dissipative structures, which emerged after the works of Ilya Prigozhin. Namely, dissipative structures, auto waves, thermodynamic parameters were accepted as analogues to many economic phenomena [1,2]. It is interesting that recently Prigozhin has applied such considerations to purely economic problems [3]. Synergy concepts have also been applied to various problems of society (economics, history, ethnology - [1,4]). Some ideas from disaster theory also have applications for interesting problems [4-6]. It is also worth mentioning the approach based on the leading equation for micro-probabilities of transition that emerged after the works of Weidlich and Haag [7,8].

Recently, ideas about the self-organization of an object (principles for the study of large systems operating on the stability boundary) have been developed for economics [9-11].

All ideas above have been applied to some extent and as analogies of the behavior of a large society. However, it should be noted that more basic laws of society are not fully understood in physical concepts and model structure.

The proposed materials describe a certain class of models and concepts that can form a universal methodological background for the systems under consideration with respect to different spatial and temporal scales and hierarchical levels. It should be noted that in our case many other ideas from different disciplines are involved - general systems theory, cybernetics, computer science and ... philosophical-humanities. The author hopes that the proposed concept developed since the early 90's will serve as a successful implementation of all such ideas.

1.1. Spatial and time scales and hierarchical structure of the society

As the author suggests, the problems in the title of this subsection can also be considered in accordance with the proposed methodology. First of all, we should make some remarks about time scales in the society structure. The common place now is that there are many periodic phenomena in history. Many periods are known in the economy: cycles of Kondratyev (approximately 50 years), Blacksmith (15-20 years) in construction, Cameron (150-300) (see works by Glazyev, Firsov, Marchetti, Schumpeter). At the same time, there are periodic processes in social and political life. The most recognized is fashion in clothes. The following example is given by election processes in stable societies (such as in the USA). It is known that in the USA there is a cycle of the period of 16-years in interest of a society to scientific and abstract knowledge or on the contrary interest to business and personal success (see for example works of A. Schlesinger). The next period in history is the period of global change in world history. It is recognized that the leading countries in history were successively Spain-England-Germany-USA with a period of change of 150 - 300 years [17]. According to L. Gumilev, the typical time of existence of nations is about 800 years. Much larger historical scales - scales of development of world religions - the axis of history (with periods of approximately 2000 years, according to Jasper). In addition to periodic processes, many aperiodic (and stochastic) processes have now been recognized. Such processes cause chaos and take place in many areas - financial, economic, weather forecasts [3, 18].

Another important aspect is the essentially hierarchical nature of society. Society has (very schematically) elements and connections between them. Some comments related to the hierarchies in society are required. We can consider as elements not only individuals but also factories, organizations, branches of industry, elements of nature and so on. Of course, the procedure of aggregation of parts can combine some "elementary" level objects into elements of a higher level. For example, you can consider factories, branches of industry, individual countries as elements obtained by combining the parts - A. Petrov and A. Shananin considered some aggregation procedures in economics. There are many possibilities to combine elements into blocks and levels. We can also consider a hierarchy of levels and basic elements as a complex object.

1.2. Internal image of the world and mentality of personality

There are also many concepts and problems considered in philosophy, political science, sociology and which have no adequate analogues in system theory. Examples: the reflexivity of society (N. Luman's reference systems themselves), G. Homans's theory of social exchange, the individual model of Mira Y. Habermas or P. Chikeland (see the term "Weltanschauung"), J. Kelly's individual constructs, predictive properties of society, and many others. Also important problems are the interdisciplinary concept and synthesis of sciences. And last but not least, the application of forecasts for new areas of interest. For such applications it is necessary to have detailed scenarios of the future.

For this purpose it is desirable to have an opportunity to describe such concepts as mentality, faith, emotion, preference and so on. Different scientific disciplines mentioned in the previous section have different approaches to such problems. But so far, this description has been applied only to small groups of people and mainly in the verbal or qualitative sense, due to a lack of operational methodology for quantitative reviews. Of course, there is sometimes a more developed description.

First of all, we should mention the well-known concepts from psychology - the personal constructs of J. Kelly and the repertoire grids of Franzella and Bannister. In such approaches people have been described in some (perhaps binary) scales of preference: individualism - collectivity, reforms - preservation, and so on. The second approach is the so-called cognitive maps with the description of a person as a oriented graph with key concepts of the vertex type and relations as elements of a diagram. Such a description of leaders can be found in the works of Olker, Stylos and Grompos and others. Recently, a new concept of artificial society of artificial agents has been introduced. An overview of this approach is given in [19]. There is also some verbal description of the outside world in the humanities. We should mention the concept "Weltanschauung" in Habermas, the world in Chickelland. Among others, we mention the "mental space" to describe the mentality of the people of Fokonnier, and a description of cognition with the help of some language in the works of Dijk, the social space in Bourdier. See also the concept of three worlds - physical, human and ideas by K. Popper.

Next, models of the individual with internal structure and activity are proposed. In this case, individual built-in models for the dynamics of mental parameters can be applied: neural networks, fuzzy cognitive maps, or expert systems.

1.3 Future scenarios, bifurcations and decision making

Such concepts can help in discussions about the predictability of historical processes. There are many concepts of the Philosophy of History. Examples are 1) the tendency of deterioration from the "golden era" to the present state (Plato, Popper), 2) the tendency of evolution from a bad state to a better one (Fukuyama), 3) the predictability of history and "social design" (Marxism, B. Banati), 4) anti-historism and complete unpredictability of history (K. Popper), 4) theological approach (T. Sharden). It should be noted that progress is not an absolute concept and depends on a point of view. Examples: Belorussia, life of northern tribes and aborigines.

Closely related problems are problems of chance in history, the role of the individual in history, possible and impossible ways of the historical process, virtual history and possible scenarios of history. Essentially different concepts have appeared in philosophy, historical sciences, theology concerning these questions. Recently, some of the aspects have been described qualitatively based on theories of catastrophes and bifurcations. It should be noted that now the concept of scenarios has also become one of the main instrumental tools - for example, strategic planning in economics (see review [20]).

The problems of this subsection are also related to the study of the decision-making process, which was also one of the key topics at conferences on operations research (see [16]). And the general trend in the study of decision making is a study of the internal structure of the decision maker (see [16]).

But in general, such problems are common and recognized by all. One of their main sources is the need to understand the place and role of an intellectual agent with free choice in history. Interesting considerations about the place of a person in history were given in [21]. For example, a quote on human nature from [21], Part VII: "At every moment I have many opportunities. I can do this and that. If I make one choice, then at the next moment there will be event A, if I make another, then it will be B. ...A person has to define what he has to do in the future. This must define what he has decided to be. And from Part IX: "This life may be different, ... but it becomes exactly this life," "Historical thinking ... is to consider what happened to man. Note that from the perspective of the author of this work, this may be directly related to the modeling of internal structure and foresight in society.

2. Some research problems and properties of society

First of all, we will very briefly recall some key properties of society, which should be presented in the proposed concept and models. Here we collect only some (incomplete) list of key facts and concepts from different fields of science (more details and motivations are given in the works of the author [12-16]. Such an overview will be useful for discussing some analogies in the following sections of the work.

2.1. The doctrine of life unity and abiotic environment

Until now, various scientific disciplines have addressed various subsystems of society (and regions). Now the situation is completely changing. Multiple links between states cause the appearance of a new object - the whole world as a unique global system. There is a long history of development of this concept in different areas: in economics - the World - system analysis (I. Wallerstein), in culturology - global culture (R. Robertson), in ecology - D. McNair, L. Brown, D. Odum, and the concept of sustainable development.

2.2. Civilization in Social History

At present, there is no formal description of civilization in the sense of M. Weber, A. Toynbee, S. Huntington and many others. But the concept of civilization or economic formation or regimes implicitly exists in all the above concepts. There are some models for World in System Dynamics (J. Forrester, D. Meadows and their followers), F. Marchetti, some models of the expert type, and several other more local models for private problems (L. Richardson, W. Weidlich, many macroeconomic models, etc.). But these models also cannot provide answers to all questions.

2.3. Dynamic essence of society

There is another main feature of the state of the modern world: its evolutionary character. This in modern conditions causes an obvious acceleration of changes, so that now the problems of studying the essence of global systems have become more and more complex. Therefore, the applicability of existing theories and models of society is in question. For example, there are many economic theories based on equilibrium or quasi-equilibrium concepts (W. Pareto, D. Gale, D. Keynes, P. Samuelson, L. Valras, J. Nash and others). These theories have had many brilliant achievements, but now that too many changes are taking place in the world, they are also in question. The economy now also recognizes the need to take into account global changes and ongoing changes in economic structures (e.g., J. Foster, Evolutionary Economics, 1987, many articles in magazines such as Methoduth, Esonomical Journal and so on). One of the main tools for properties research - an approach from physical theories - comes from synergetic and self-organization theory (I. Prigozhin, H. Hacken, G. Nicholis and many others). There are many achievements in the application of such concepts in the humanities (for example, see the description of the role of nonlinear and chaotic dynamics in economics: K. Lorentz, J. Schenkman, G. Mosekilde). But to date, the difficulties in building a theory of this type are still significant.

2.4. Relationships and the property of holography: K. Lorentz, J. Schenkman, G. Mozekilde

There are some basic elements in a developed society. Namely, there are many interconnections between elements of social systems (and not only in social systems, but also in natural systems). In philosophy and theology there is always the idea of interconnections of all things in the world (without specification of such influences). But in the sections of the global sciences there are usually more developed concepts to describe interrelationships, sometimes even quantitative ones. One source of the idea of interconnection is the sciences of humanity (humanities): sociology, psychology, political science and so on. Almost all known modern sociological theories have as their main ideas different types: social interactions: T. Parsons, D. Easton, E. Durkheim, social fields - K. Levin. The influence of the environment on an individual is presented in the psychology of small groups (with some scales for measuring mutual influence between individuals), implicitly in the social psychology of G. Levin. Lebon, C. Jung, G. Tard, S. Moskovichi, in Durkheim's theory of social harmony and many others.

A common phenomenon now is the recognition of the influence of the mass media. It should be noted that one of the main ones is the theory of social influence of Y. Habermas, and the theory of social exchange of D. Jung. Homans's theory of social exchange. Thus, different information flows between agents, different relations of influence energy and so on are discussed there.

Another important property of society is the integer/subsystem relationship. Many subsystems of society imitate common properties of society. For example, a small village has many common properties in relation to a country as a whole. Examples are faith, tradition, technology, education and many other things. In addition, a small part of the population can try to reproduce the structure of the initial social infrastructure in any circumstances. As an example, let us cite the behavior

2.5. Internal image of the world and mentality of personality

There are also many concepts and problems considered in philosophy, political science, sociology and which have no adequate analogues in system theory. Examples: the reflexivity of society (N. Luman's reference systems themselves), G. Homans's theory of social exchange, the individual model of Mira Y. Habermas or P. Chikeland (see the term "Weltanschauung"), J. Kelly's individual constructs, predictive properties of society, and many others. Also important problems are the interdisciplinary concept and synthesis of sciences. And last but not least, the application of forecasts for new areas of interest. For such applications it is necessary to have detailed scenarios of the future.

For this purpose it is desirable to have an opportunity to describe such concepts as mentality, faith, emotion, preference and so on. Different scientific disciplines mentioned in the previous section have different approaches to such problems. But so far, this description has been applied only to small groups of people and mainly in the verbal or qualitative sense, due to a lack of operational methodology for quantitative reviews. Of course, there is sometimes a more developed description.

First of all, we should mention the well-known concepts from psychology - the personal constructs of J. Kelly and the repertoire grids of Franzella and Bannister. In such approaches people have been described in some (perhaps binary) scales of preference: individualism - collectivity, reforms - preservation, and so on. The second approach is the so-called cognitive maps with the description of a person as a oriented graph with key concepts of the vertex type and relations as elements of a diagram. Such a description of leaders can be found in the works of Olker, Stylos and Grompos and others. Recently, a new concept of artificial society of artificial agents has been introduced. An overview of this approach is given in [19]. There is also some oral description of the outside world in the humanities. We should mention the concept "Weltanschauung" in Habermas, the world in Chickelland. Among others, we mention the "mental space" to describe the mentality of the people of Fokonnier, and a description of cognition with the help of some language in the works of Dijk, the social space in Bourdier. See also the concept of three worlds - physical, human and ideas by K. Popper.

Next, models of the individual with internal structure and activity are proposed. In this case, individual built-in models for the dynamics of mental parameters can be applied: neural networks, fuzzy cognitive maps, or expert systems.

2.6 Future scenarios, bifurcations and decision making

Such concepts can help in discussions about the predictability of historical processes. There are many concepts of the Philosophy of History. Examples are 1) the tendency of deterioration from the "golden era" to the present state (Plato, Popper), 2) the tendency of evolution from a bad state to a better one (Fukuyama), 3) the predictability of history and "social design" (Marxism, B. Banati), 4) anti-historism and complete unpredictability of history (K. Popper), 4) theological approach (T. Sharden). It should be noted that progress is not an absolute concept and depends on a point of view. Examples: Belorussia, life of northern tribes and aborigines.

Closely related problems are problems of chance in history, the role of the individual in history, possible and impossible ways of the historical process, virtual history and possible scenarios of history. Essentially different concepts have appeared in philosophy, historical sciences, theology concerning these questions. Recently, some of the aspects have been described qualitatively based on theories of catastrophes and bifurcations. It should be noted that now the concept of scenarios has also become one of the main instrumental tools - for example, strategic planning in economics (see review [20]).

The problems of this subsection are also related to the study of the decision-making process, which was also one of the key topics at conferences on operations research (see [16]). And the general trend in the study of decision making is a study of the internal structure of the decision maker (see [16]).

But in general, such problems are common and recognized by all. One of their main sources is the need to understand the place and role of an intellectual agent with free choice in history. Interesting considerations about the place of a person in history were given in [21]. For example, a quote on human nature from [21], Part VII: "At every moment I have many opportunities. I can do this and that. If I make one choice, then at the next moment there will be event A, if I make another, then it will be B. ...A person has to define what he has to do in the future. This must define what he has decided to be. And from Part IX: "This life may be different, ... but it becomes exactly this life," "Historical thinking ... is to consider what happened to man. Note that from the perspective of the author of this work, this may be directly related to the modeling of internal structure and foresight in society.

REFERENCES

1. Puu T. Atractors, Bifurcations &Chaos. Nonlinear Mathematics in Economics. Berlin: Springel- Verlag, 2000

2. Watts D.J., Strogatz S. Collective dynamics of "small- world" networks // Nature. 1998. Vol.393. pp.440-442.

3. Prigogine I. The Networked Society // J.World- Syst.Res. 2000. Vol. 6, No.3. pp. 892-898.

4. Капица С., Курдюмов С., Малинецкий Г. Синергетика и прогнозы будущего. М.: Наука, 1997. [in Russian]

5. Лотман Ю. Семиосфера. СПб: Искусство, 2000. 740 с. [in Russian]

6. Bullard J., Butler A. Nonlinearity and chaos in economic models: implications for policy decisions // The economical Journal. 1993. Vol.103. pp.849- 867.

7. Weidlich W., Haag G. Concepts and Models of a Quantitative Sociology. The Dynamics of Interacting Populations. Berlin: Springer- Verlag, 1983.

8. Troitzsch K. Simulation and Structuralism // Modelling and Simulation in the Social Sciences from the Science Point of View / R.Hegselmann et. al. eds, Kluwer, 1996. pp. 183- 207.

9. Bak P., Sneppen K. Punctated Equilibrium and Criticality in a Simple model of evolution // Phys.Rev.Lett. 1993. Vol.71, No.24, pp.4083- 4089.

10. Ponzi A., Aizava Y. Criricality and punctated equilibrium in a spin systems model of a financial market // Chaos, Solitons& Fractals, 2000. Vol.11, pp.1739- 1746.

11. Stanley H., Amaral L., Canning D., Gopikrishnan P., Lee Y., Liu Y. Econophisics: can physicists contribute to the science of economics? // Physica A, 1999. Vol. 269, No. 1. Pp. 156- 169.

12. Макаренко А. О моделях глобальных социо- экономических процессов // Доклады Украинской Академии Наук, 1994. No.12.c.85- 87. [in Russian]

13. Makarenko A. New Neuronet Models of Global Socio- Economical Processes // Gaming /Simulation for Policy Development and Organisational Change / J.Geurts, C.Joldersma, E.Roelofs eds, Tillburg: Tillburg University Press, 1998. Pp. 128- 132.

14. Makarenko A. (2000) Models with anticipatory property for large socio-

economical systems // Proc. 16 th World Congress of IMACS, Lausanna, 21-25 August, Switzerland, 2000. Paper n. 422-1. 10 pp.

15. Макаренко А. Многозначніе нейросети и проблемы их математического исследования // Резюме 5 й Межд. Мат.Школы: Метод функции Ляпунова и его приложение. Симферополь: СГУ, 2000. С.116. [in Russian]

16. Abstracts of 18 th Eoropean Conference on Operational Research, Rotterdam, Holland, 9-12 July 2001.

17. Wallerstine I., The Heritage of Sociology, The Promise of Social Science // Presidental Addres, XIV th World Congress of Sociology, Montreal, July 26, 1998, Part 2. http://fbc.binghampton.edu/iwprad2.htm

18. Loskutov A., Michailov A. Introduction to synergetics. Vol.2. Berlin: Springer- Verlag, 1998.

19. Wooldrige M., Jennings N. Agent Theories, Architectures. and Languages: A Survey // Proceed. of the 1994 Workshop on Agent Theories, Architectures, and Languages. Berlin: Springer-Verlag, 1995. pp.1-29.

20. Liebl, F. Rethiking Trends - And How to Link Them to Scenarious // Abstracts book Conf. EURO 18. Rotterdam, Holland, 9-12 July. 2001.

21. Ortega y Gasset Jose, Histiria como sistema. Obras completas, 3-a ed. Madrid, 1955. Vol.4. p.9-69. (In Spain).

CHAPTER III

MENTALITY ISSUES IN THE TRANSFORMATION PROCESSES OF THE POSTMODERNITY SOCIETY

The issues of conscious transformation of large socio-economic-political systems are becoming increasingly important in modern conditions, both in theoretical and practical terms. It should be noted that in the Ukrainian context they are particularly significant in terms of governing the country in conditions of great challenges, as well as internal and external uncertainty. When considering these issues there is a need for adequate understanding and consideration of modern stage of society evolution, namely the postmodern state [1, 2]. Put simply, this state is characterized by coexistence of different types of society subsystems, pluralism of thoughts, rules, morals, stages of development, etc.

Different concepts, approaches, definitions and methodologies to the problem of sustainable development, especially in the global aspect, can be considered as one of the examples [3, 4]. Of course, material factors play crucial role in consideration of social systems: resources, effect of environment, technological wave, infrastructure and many others.

It is obvious that human properties as a thinking being are very important (and perhaps even outstanding). Figuratively speaking it can be called the human mentality. In terms of an individual, these issues are considered by psychology, neurophysiology, computational neuroscience and philosophy. The next very important step is to understand the social systems as groups of interacting entities. In this case, it is possible to talk about systems of a large number of thinking agents with different mental properties. Many issues have already been considered by various disciplines related to society: social science, political science, economics, theory of public administration, social psychology, cultural studies, theory of management and many others. However, it is now becoming increasingly clear that quantity, quality and depth of problems associated with understanding the mentality of properties is becoming increasingly necessary, even in solving the current management problems for post-industrial society in postmodernism.

Considering the existence of society archetypes is one of the examples of such a problem. As it is known, the history of those concepts begins with already classical works of C. Jung [5, 6], it has gone a long way of development (e.g., S.

Grof [7]) and continues now [8]. In particular, the Ukrainian School of Archetypes, founded by E. Afonin [9, 10], should be noted. Very figuratively, according to these sources, the archetypes include deep constructions in the subconscious (which are often not understood by individuals) that are inherent in social communities, very stable and are transmitted from generation to generation. For example, behavioral stereotypes are often such constructs. It is intuitively clear what such constructs are. But it is still very difficult to formalize, measure, or apply them in real-world management. It should be noted that approach of psychological tests, including color, developed by E. Afonin and his colleagues [11], is one of the interesting approaches to the study of these concepts (let's say to the measurement). The problems of global sustainable development are another example of problems where mentalities are important [3, 4].

Despite the great attention to sustainable development at all levels — from the world leaders to the population of different countries — it is recognized that significant changes from economic to environmental way are still ahead. We can assume that the main thing in such changes and transformational processes will be carried out in the future. The change in rules, preferences and attitudes of society is the main obstacle to sustainable development. These very concepts are related to and based on understanding of mental properties of the person. Therefore, the problem of sustainable development requires an adequate understanding of influence of properties of mentality, including archetypes.

Purpose of the chapter. So far, the influence of mentality of individuals on processes in society has been largely studied using the methods of the humanities, that is, intuitively and qualitatively. At the same time, it is well known that increasing use of methods of the exact sciences, especially mathematics and physics, is the mainstream of development of various sciences. It should be noted that the author proposed the aspects of mathematical modeling of society, which allow us to formalize and include the issues of mentality and to carry out the modeling, including formulation of real management plans. That is the subject of the proposed Chapter.

1. Analysis of recent research and publications. Consideration of mental properties of subjects of large social systems

Some problems and properties of society.
First of all, we will very briefly recall some key properties of society that should be presented in the proposed conception and models (a large number of details

and motivations are given in the author's works [12, 13]). Here below we remember title some points from Chapter II which are useful for mentality consideration,

Doctrine of unity of life and abiotic environments.
Civilization in social history.
Dynamic essence of the society.
Relationships and property of holoraphicity.
Spatial and time scales and hierarchical structure of society.
Internal image of the world and mentality of the individual.
Scenarios for the future, bifurcation and decision-making.

2. Verbal description of some basic materials

Thus, in the previous sections, the author outlined some concepts related to modern society. The analysis of the problems above and many others led the author to a new class of models. These models resemble models with associative memory in artificial neural networks. The details of models and motivations for their introduction are given in other works [12, 13] and will be presented in Part II of this book. Therefore, here we will describe verbally only main features of simple models and emphasize some points related to the properties of predicting, multiplicity and some quantum and mechanical concepts.

2.1 Models

Let's imagine a society consisting of a large number of individuals and let each individual be characterized by a state vector with a set of possible values. There are many possibilities to connect the elements into blocks and levels in such models. In a highly developed society, the individuals have many complex relations. Let's formalize this. We assume that there are relations between the individuals. In this way, the set of elements and relations characterizes the state of society. The analysis of recent models for environments from the sets of elements and relationships shows the similarity of such models of society with neural network models.

The hierarchical systems can be described in the same way. We can assume first that there are M hierarchical levels in the social and economic system with elements at j-th level. Each i-th element at j-th level has a description with a parameter vector. Some elements at the selected levels may be in dependencies marked by a set of possible indexes in the dependencies. Many elements in a developed society have a large number of connections at upper and lower levels.

The other processes of interest (political, social, educational, etc.) have a similar network presentation and society is a combination of such networks.

The relations can be very different in nature. The meaning of relations can represent the normalization of economic, informational, management channels, national, family, professional interactions and others. The society is an evolutionary system with dynamic changes over time. Further, for simplicity, we consider only discrete models with moments of time: $0, 1, 2, \ldots \ldots, n, \ldots \ldots$ Following the evolutionary nature of systems, we believe that it is naturally to consider the values of parameters at this point in time as a system input at time n and the value at the next $(n + 1)$ moment (for $n = 0, 1, 2, \ldots$) as an output. It should be noted that the set of elements can change in a developing society. For example, in the economy, the list of companies and corporations is constantly changing due to bankruptcies and coalitions. The social, political and government networks are also often transformed. This generally leads to changes in the number of elements N (n) and number of hierarchical levels M (n) at different points in time.

The author's models consider society as a large complex object created from many elements with connections. Consideration the properties of society allows us to select some interesting properties and then proposes models that can mimic the regimes of society. In a strange way, the models resemble the models of brain activity — neural network. The author has been studied such models since 1992 and has already had some interesting applications.

We now briefly describe the models. The first step of model development is to select the model elements and describe them. As the mentality of the population should be taken into account, the individuals with description of their qualities (mental and other: economic, demographic and other parameters) were taken as elements. These parameters can be evaluated in some psychological scales, in social science and other humanities (see, for example, the mental spaces of Fauconnier, set grids of Kelly, etc.).

A critical step in creation of new models is to take into account the concept of global culture of society as collection of all material achievements plus spiritual, such as morality, ethics, religion, justice and creation. The global culture is also sometimes called the collective memory of society. The global culture is a very stable structure and is the basis of civilization (A. Toynbee, I. Wallerstein). The proposed models have the dynamic principles that allow us to model the behavior of global culture over time. This is due to the fact that models have the property of associative memory. The behavior of historical processes resembles the desire for very stable structures, the so-called points of attraction in the image recognition in computer science and neuroscience. It is important that many social subsystems in society also have similar properties, and this allows us to consider the selected submodels.

In earlier works, the author considered a new class of social models as a modification of Hopfield neural network models or spin glasses. It is known that the dynamics of Hopfield model is derived from consideration of the functional that is called "energy". In Hopfield models, the system tends to one of some stable states with a minimum of energy functional. Many of possible initial conditions result in a small number of such minimum "energy" states that are called points of attraction. It should be reminded that such a law is valid only in case of symmetric connections.

In the simplest case, the model takes the form of famous Hopfield model presented in many publications. In case of hierarchical systems and symmetric connections, there is also a functional — analog of "energy" between different elements and different levels.

3. Models with internal structure and mentality

3.1 Internal representation of the external world

Considering the mentality requires consideration of internal structures and their inclusion in the global hierarchical models. There are many approaches to considering the mentality. The most natural way is to consider the model for the internal structure also in the class of neural networks. The easiest way is to represent the image of the World in the brain or the individual in the model as a collection of elements and connections between elements. In this image of the world, there is a place to represent the individual directly with personal faith, skills, knowledge and advantages. We imagined some individual with some perception of structure of the World. This perception is similar to the "pattern" above. The substantially new effect is that the individual can present himself as one of the elements of the "pattern". The mental structures of other personalities are also represented in the same way. Thus, society as a complex system has its own new representation. At the first level of description, we have collection of elements connected by links. At the second level of description, the structure (some image of the world) is added to all elements.

3.2 One possible way to consider the mentality

The laws for elemental dynamics should depend on such a representation. To represent the image of the external World in the individual brain: it is very important that each individual has his or her own personal image of the World. Some of the simplest options will be presented in the next section, in parallel with description of the property of predicting. Of course, there can also be the recursion with many levels of recursion, as in the theory of reflexive systems of N. Luhmann, G. Soros, S. Lefebvre and others. In our scheme, this can be represented as a mutual representation of all personalities in the internal representation of the individual.

3.3 Internal representation of the external world

Considering the mentality requires consideration of internal structures and their inclusion in the global hierarchical models. There are many approaches to considering the mentality. The most natural way is to consider the model for the internal structure also in the class of neural networks. The neural network models were initially introduced when studying the brain. First, we can change the basic laws. At the phenomenological level, this can be implemented by introducing the subdivision of element parameters into external and internal variables and setting separate laws for two parameter blocks — external and internal output and input parameters. The functions can be of completely different forms. For example, the equations for external variables can be in the form of neural networks combined with differential equations for internal variables. Let's make a very important remark that allows, in principle, a significant summary of the proposed methodology and models, including the problems of archetypes, sustainable development, transformation and other similar problems. The internal variables should be divided into two classes. The first class includes variables that change relatively quickly in dynamics under the influence of environment and internal state of the individual. In fact, most of the current economic tasks deal with such variables (and external factors). The second class includes relatively stable variables, which include perception, archetypes, development patterns, etc. These constructs can also change but much slower (for example, at change of several generations).

The parameters of the first and second classes are just what should be considered as components of the mentality. One of the most promising ways to consider the mentality is to find the equation in the neural network class. The easiest way is to represent the image of the World in the brain of the individual or in the model as a collection of elements and connections between elements. In this image of the world, there is a place to represent the individual directly with personal faith, skills, knowledge and advantages. It is interesting that the importance of "pictures", "patterns" and others is widely introduced in the works of G. Durand [14]. The schematic perception of the image of the world of the individual can be presented in the proposed scheme.

The representation of an individual is important. He has a certain perception of structure of the World. This perception is similar to the "pattern" and is represented as networks. The substantially new effect is that the individual can present himself as one of the elements of the "pattern". The mental structures of other personalities are also represented in the same way. Thus, society as a complex system has new representation. At the first level of description, we have collection of elements connected by links. At the second level of description, the structure (some image of the world) is added to all elements.

The laws for elemental behavior should depend on such a perception. Formally, we can introduce the projection operators P to represent the image of the external world in the individual brain: it is very important that each individual has his or her own personal image of the World. It should be noted that the influence of the operator P can be divided into many local projection operators. The equation can then be replaced with a more complex one by substituting the self-representation of the individual in the right part of the dynamic law for elemental dynamic change in parameters. Some of the simplest options will be presented below, in parallel with description of the property of predicting.

Some qualitative consequences of applying the proposed methodology for modeling large social systems. Let's make a very important remark that allows, in principle, a significant summary of the proposed methodology and models, including the problems of archetypes, sustainable development, transformation and other similar problems. The internal variables should be divided into two classes. The first class includes variables that change relatively quickly in dynamics under the influence of environment and internal state of the individual. In fact, most of the current economic tasks deal with such variables (and external factors). The second class includes relatively stable variables, which include perception, archetypes, development patterns, etc. These constructs can also change but much slower (for example, at change of several generations). The parameters of the first and second classes are just what should be considered as components of the mentality.

As has already been emphasized, the second class of variables allows considering the aspects of archetypes. In particular, in the simplest case, they can be represented through use of color psychological tests in the proposed models [11] and through introduction of special parameters (or even one summarized parameter).

The proposed methodology is also suitable for consideration of global problem of sustainable development. The idea of "economic" and "environmental" way of society evolution can in fact also be represented as constructs in terms of variables of the second class, that is, as quasi-stable constructs. Therefore, the transition from "economic" to "environmental" way depends on changing the leading constructs of individuals. This will sooner or later happen through education, media influence and other.

It can also be assumed that in the future the proposed conception will also be useful for practical tasks of public administration. At first, the conception can give a qualitative understanding of influence of various factors (including archtypical) on processes in society. Also, with further development and working out in detail the proposed models, they can become part of state decision-making systems.

It is obvious that in decision-making the individuals have predictions for the future. In this case, the states of elements in the model should depend on the images of the future described in the internal view. According to [15], we call this case hyperincursion. The selection procedure is another important part of forestalling.

It should be noted that the proposed conceptions allow us to move towards an adequate reflection of modern conceptions of postmodern society, for example, the phenomenon of emergence of simplified crowds of society studied by M. Mafussali [16].

The system of equations and its modifications can be the basis for study of many problems with internal and external images of the world. We should emphasize that the right part of the equation depends on the future values of the state of the element. This form is opposite to the form of delayed equations. It is very promising that the structure of such a system coincides in structure with caution systems studied by D. Dubois [15]. This entails possible similarity in properties.

Conclusions

In the proposed chapter we outlined the part of the approach to process modeling in large social systems. It was suggested to include the properties of mentality of individuals in society, as well as the individuals' property of predicting in a rigorous approach. As a result, we obtained some new models considering the properties of mentality of individual. The possibility of including the archetypical problems in the mathematical models is also described. The possibilities of applying the conceptions to problems of society management are also proposed. The approach useful for application in the economic models are proposed.

REFERENCES

1. Lyotard, J.-P. (1984). The Postmodern Condition: A report on Knowledge. Minneapolis: Univ. of Minnesota Pres [in English].
2. Aylesworth, G. (2013). Postmodernism. The Stanford Encyclopedia of Philosophy. E. N. Zalta (Ed.). Retrieved from https://plato.stanford. edu/archives/sum2013/entries/postmodernism/ [in English].
3. Daly, H. (2014). From Uneconomic Growth to a Steady State Economy. Advanced in Ecological Economics. Chetlenham [in English].
4. Makarenko, A. (2018). Formalization, Modeling and Anticipatory Properties in Computational Science for Sustainable Development. Electronic Preprint of EWG-ORD 2018 Workshop OR for Sustainable Development. Madrid [in English].
5. Jung, C. G. (1968). The Archetypes and The Collective Unconscious. (2 ed.). Princeton: Bollingen [in English].
6. Afonin, E. A. Martynov, A. Yu. (2016). Arkhetypni zasady modeliuvannia sotsialnykh protsesiv [Archetypal principles of social process modeling]. Problemy uriaduvannia – Governance problems, 2(3), 34-47 [in Ukrainian].
7. Grof, S. (1994). Za predelamy mozga [Beyond the Brain: Birth, Death, and Transcendence in Psychotherapy]. Moscow [in Russian].
8. Stevens, A. (1999). On Jung: Updated Edition. (2nd ed.). Princeton: Princeton University Press [in English].
9. Sushii, O. V., Plakhtii, T. O. Afonin, E. A. (2017). Arkhetepika i publichne upravlinnia: stratehii ta mekhanizmy rozviazannia konfliktiv u suchasnomu sviti [Archetypics and Public Management: Strategies and Mechanisms for Conflict Resolution in the Modern World]. Ukrainskyi sotsium – Ukrainian society, 2, 146-157 [in Ukrainian].
10. htpp://usarch.org/
11. Afonin, E. (2006). Color and Psyche. Airport, 1, 54-55 [in English].
12. Makarenko, A. (1998). New Neuronet Models of Global Socio- Economical Processes. Gaming / Simulation for Policy Development and Organisational Change. J. Geurts, C. Joldersma, E. Roelofs (eds.). (pp. 128-132). Tillburg: Tillburg University Press [in English].
13. Makarenko, A. (2000). Models with anticipatory property for large socioeconomical systems. // Proc. 16 th World Congress of IMACS, Lausanna, 21–25 August, Switzerland, 2000. Paper n. 422-1. 10 p.
14. Durand G. Les Structures anthropologiques de l'imaginaire, Paris, Dunod (first edition, Paris, P.U.F., 1960). 15. Dubois D. Introduction to computing

Anticipatory Systems // Int.J. of Comput. Anticip. Syst, (Liege), 1998. Vol. 2, pp. 3–14.

16. Maffesoli M., La Connaissance ordinaire – Précis de sociologie compréhensive, 1985, Paris, Librairie des Méridiens; rééd. 2007, Paris, Klincks

PART 2

MATHEMATICAL CONCEPTS AND MODELS

CHAPTER IV

MODELS OF SOCIETY FOR SUSTAINABLE DEVELOPMENT

Taking into account all the discussions given above, now it is possible to return more specifically to the mathematical modeling of SD. Clearly, the global SD problem is very complex and multidimensional, with many 'pillars', variable processes, systems, hierarchies of levels, scales, etc. Recently the development of mathematical modeling took place in such a way that, first, models for specific clearly identified problem areas (for example, heat conductivity, elasticity, contamination propagation, molecular structure, biology of populations, etc.) were most developed. Therefore, when building global SD models for individual pillars, subsystems, processes, it is possible (and, thus, desirable) to use ready-made or well-adapted models. However, there are problems of adequate coupling of such models in the integral model complex. By the way, we note that the general definition (or rather the description of the global SD) can help in the selection and coupling of models. True, the resulting integrated model, composed of different types of models, can therefore be very difficult to model (even with super-powerful computers), and the results are very complex in their interpretations. Therefore, any attempts to construct integral models (especially with new principles of construction) can be extremely useful. Below, we present the basis for constructing global models of SD, built on new principles, that allow to consider qualitatively and quantitatively nontrivial questions such as mentality, scenarios, punctuated equilibrium, system transformation, etc.

1. Models of society for SD in the class of models with associated memory

The basic basic principles were developed by the author, starting from the 1990s (for references Makarenko 1994 [20], 1998 [23], 2002 [18], 2013 [19]). Here we give only a squeeze out of the main ideas of the approach, as well as some details of the development of models and approaches, as well as some ways of developing SD models and modeling SD. Imagine a society consisting of $N \gg 1$ personalities and let each individual be characterized by a state vector

$S_i = \{s_1^i, ..., s_{k_i}^i, s^i{}_{k_i+1}, ...$, $s_l^i \in M_l^i, l = 1, ..., M_i$ where M_i^l is a set of possible

values s_i. There are many opportunities to compose elements, blocks and levels in such models. In sufficiently developed societies, individuals have many complex connections. We formalize this. We assume that there are connections

between personalities i and j. Let J_{ij}^{pq} be the connection between the p

components of the element i and the q components of the element j. Thus, the

set $Q = (\{s_i\}, \{J_{ij}^{pq}\}, i, j = 1, 2, ... N)$ characterizes the state of society (Fig. 1).

Analysis of recent models for environments from sets of elements and relationships shows the similarity of such models of society and neural network models.

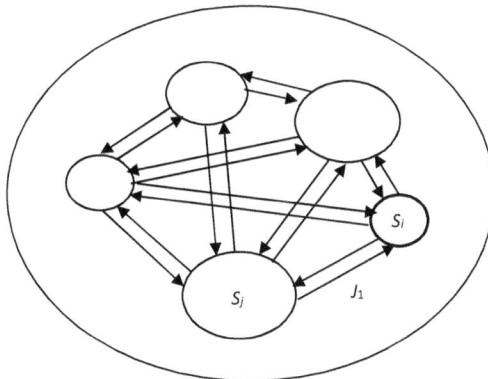

Fig. 1. Sample pattern of Q description in the simplest model

Similarly, hierarchical systems can be described. We can initially assume that there are M hierarchical levels in the socio-economic system with $N(j)$ elements at the j-th level. Each i-th element at the j-th level has a description with the parameter vector. Q_i^j, $i=1,2,...N_j),j=1,2..M$. Some elements $Q=(\{s_i\},\{J_{ij}^{pq}\}, i,j=1,2,...N)$ at the selected levels can be in the dependencies marked with a set of possible indexes in the dependencies $L_i^j \subset \{1,2,...N_j\}$. Many elements in a developed society have a vast number of compounds on the upper and lower levels. Note that other processes of interest (political, social, educational, etc.) have a similar network representation and society, on the whole pattern of Q description in the simplest model. Links can be very different in nature. The values of links can represent the formalization of economic, information, management channels, national, family, professional and so on interactions. Society is an evolutionary system with dynamic changes in time. Further, for simplicity we consider only discrete models with time moments: 0,1,2,...,n,... . Following the evolutionary nature of systems, we believe that it is natural to treat both the input of the system at the moment of time n of the parameter values at this instant of time and as the output of the value at the next moment $(n+1)$ (for $n=0,1,2,...$). Note that in a developing society, the content of a set of elements can vary. For example, in the economy, the list of firms and corporations changes constantly with bankruptcies and the creation of coalitions. Social, political, governmental networks are also often transformed. This leads generally to a change in the number of elements $N(n)$ and the number of hierarchical levels $M(n)$ at different instants of time. Models of the author view society as a large complex object, created from many elements with connections. Consideration of the properties of society allows you to choose some interesting properties and then offer models that can mimic the modes of society. Surprisingly, models resemble models of brain activity – neural networks (Haykin 1994 [13]). Such models have been studied by the author since 1992 and already had some interesting applications. Now let us briefly describe the model. The first step in developing a model is to select model elements and describe them. Since it is required to take into account the mentality of the population, individuals were selected for the elements with a description of their qualities (mental and other: economic, demographic and other parameters). These parameters can be evaluated in some psychological scales, in sociology and other humanities (see for example the mental spaces of G. Fauconnier, the lattice of the repertoire sets of J. Kelly).

A critical step in creating new models is to take into account the notions of the global culture of society as a collection of all material achievements plus spiritual types of morality, ethics, religion, justice, education. Global culture is also sometimes called the collective memory of society. Global culture is a very stable construction and forms the basis of civilization (A. Toynbee, I. Wallerstein) – see (Wallerstein 1998 [37]). Dynamic principles of proposed models allow modeling the behavior of a global culture in time. This is due to the fact that models have the property of associative memory. The behavior of historical processes resembles the desire for very stable structures and socalled points of attraction (attractors) in pattern recognition in informatics and neurobiology. It is important that many social subsystems in society also have similar properties, and this allows us to consider individual sub-models. In earlier works, the author considered a new class of models of society as a modification of models of the type of neural network Hopfield models or spin glasses (Haykin 1994 [13]; Sutton et al. 1988 [34]). It is known that the dynamics of the Hopfield model is derived from a consideration of a functional called "energy":

$$E = \sum_{i \neq j}^{N} J_{ij} s_i s_j, \tag{1}$$

where {+1,–1} are possible states of elements in the network, N – number of elements, J_{ij} – connections between the i-th and the j-th elements. In Hopfield models, the system tends to one of the few stable states with a minimum of functional (1). Many of possible initial conditions lead to a small number of such minimal "energy" states, called points of attraction. Potential landscape of "energy" in this case looks approximately as in Fig. 2, 3 (represented conditionally as the surface of the function from the states of the elements).

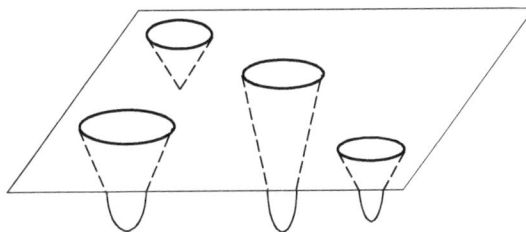

Fig. 2 Illustration of the potential "landscape" of the system

The projection of potential landscape "from above"with representing two stable minima of "energy" are represented in Fig. 3. The Fig. 4 represents the one-dimensional caricature of "energy landscape".

We recall that such a law is correct only in the symmetric case, when $J_{ij} = J_{ji}$. In more general case, the models have the form:

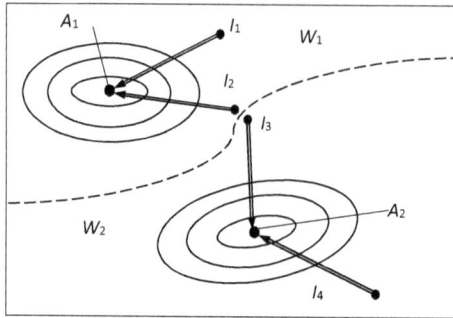

Fig. 3. The type of potential landscape "from above". The dynamic elements shown are: A_1 and A_2 - attractors of the system (in this case, point) W_1 and W_2 - attraction regions of attractors; $I_1 - I_4$ possible trajectories of ystem

$$s_i(t+1) = f_i(\{s_i(t)\}\{s_i(t-1)\},...\{J_{ij}(t-1)\},...b). \tag{2}$$

In the simplest case, the model takes the form of the well-known Hopfield model, presented in many publications, its dynamics equations have the form:

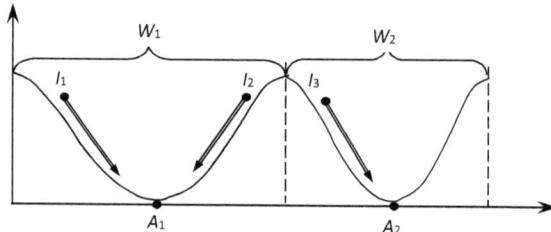

Fig.4. "One-dimensional projection" of the system

$$s_i(t+1) = \operatorname{sign}(h_i);$$

$$h_i = \sum_{j \neq i}^{N} J_{ij} s_j;$$

$$\text{sign}(W) = \{+1...\text{if}..W>0;\ -1..\text{if}..W\le0\}.,\qquad\qquad (3)$$

where W is the argument of sign function. In the case of hierarchical systems and symmetric connections between different elements and different levels, there also exist a functional – an analog of "energy" in (1).

2. Models with inner structure of nodes and account of the mentality

2.1 Internal representation of the external world

Accounting for the mentality requires consideration of internal structures and their inclusion in global hierarchical models. There are many approaches to accounting for the mentality (see an overview of some aspects in (Makarenko 2013 [19])). The most natural way to accomplish this task is to consider the model for the internal structure also in the class of neural network models. First, we can change the basic laws (2) or (3). At the phenomenological level, this can be realized by introducing a subdivision of the parameters of the elements into external Q_{ije} and internal variables Q_{ije}, Q_{iji} and establishing separate laws for two parameter blocks

$$Y_e = f_e(X_e, X_i, P, E),$$

$$Y_i = f_i(X_e, X_i, P, E).\qquad\qquad (4)$$

Here x_e, Y_e, X_i, Y_i are external and internal output and input parameters. Functions f_e and f_i can have absolutely different forms. For example, equations for external variables can take the form of neural networks, connected with differential equations for internal variables. But one of the most promising ways to account the mentality is to search analogs of equations (3) also in the neural-network class. It is proposed to introduce the builtin mental models of the World in elements that represent individuals or centers of decisionmaking with human participation. The simplest way is to represent the image of the World in the brain of the individual or in the model as a collection of elements and connections between the elements. In such an image of the world, the individual can be represented directly with his personal faith, Fig. 5

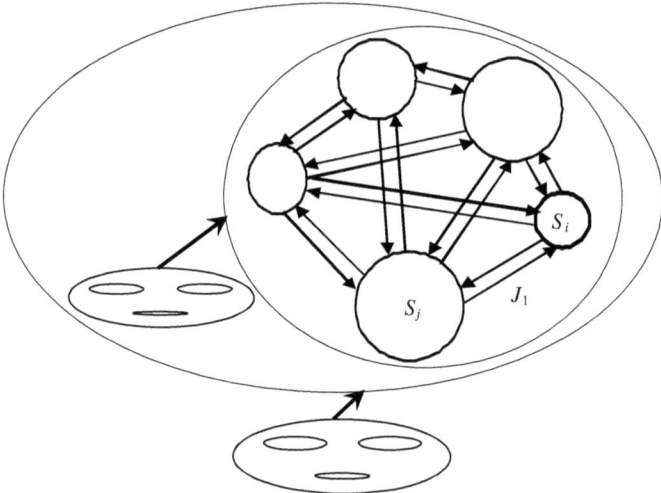

Fig. 5. Internal representation of the World of an individual

The type of potential landscape "from above" may be represented as in the Fig. 2-4. The dynamic elements are shown: A_1 and A_2 – attractors of the system (in this case, point), W_1 and W_2 – attraction regions of attractors; $I_1, ..., I_4$ – possible trajectories of the system skills, knowledge, preferences. Individual has some idea about the structure of the World. This representation is similar to the "sample" in Fig. 2. But an essentially new effect is that an individual can present himself as one of the elements of a "pattern". The mental structures of other persons can also be represented in the same way. Thus, society as a complex system has essentially a new concept. At the first level of description we have a collection of elements that are connected by links. On the second level of the description, we connect the structure (some image of the world) to all elements. At this level, the construction resembles a bundle of differential topology.

2.2 One possible way of accounting for the mentality

The laws for elemental behavior must depend on such a representation. Formally, we can introduce projection operators P to represent the image of the external world in the individual brain: it is very important that each individual has his own personal image of the World. We note that the action of the operator P can be subdivided into many local projection operators. Then equation (2) can be replaced by a more complicated one, substituting the selfrepresentation of the individual in the right-hand side of the dynamic law for the elemental dynamic variation of the parameters. Some of the simplest versions will be presented in the next section, in parallel with the description of the proactive property. Of course, there can also be a recursion with many levels of recursion, as in the theory of reflexive systems of N. Luhmann (Luhmann 1995), G. Soros (Soros 2000), V. Lefebvre (Lefebvre 1982), and so on.

The next step in developing models is to take into account the anticipatory aspects of personalities. It is obvious that individuals in the decision-making processes have predictions for the future. In this case, the states of the elements in the model must depend on the images of the future described in the internal representation. As in an ordinary reflexive system, certain stages of iteration in anticipation of the future can exist. Following Dubois 2001 [10, 11], we call such a case a hyperincursion. Another important part of prediction is the procedure of branch choice from multivalued solution. A description of the internal structure was given in the subsection 2.1. Now we give a possible structure of models which can be taken into account. First, we describe the structure of a model with one element with an internal structure. If there is no internal structure, then the system described in Section 1 for the dynamic law is suitable. For example, let the individual with an internal structure have an index (an indicator). Its dynamic law is defined by two components. The first component is determined by the external mean field as in Section 1. The second part of the dynamic law is related to the internal dynamics of the first individual. Note that this dynamic law partially explains the desire of the individual. There exist many models for such (internal) part of the dynamics. Usually the types of such models correspond to considered phenomena (economical, psychological, social etc.). In principle, each of such models can be used for accounting of mental properties of individuals. But we suppose that it is useful to use neural network type models for the purposes of building models with mentality accounting. This is due to the analogy of representation of external and internal spaces as network structure. Some discussion and examples see in (Makarenko 2002 [18], 2013 [19]; Levkov et al. 1998 [17]).

3. Scheme of application of models with associated memory to SD problem

In the previous sections, the principles of constructing models with associative memory for modeling large social systems were described. Below we discuss some possible ways on such models using in the SD problem.

3.1 General SD Circuits

Here is a description of commonly accepted illustration of SD schemes (Rogers 2007 [30]; Sheffran et al. 2012 [31]; Daly 2014 [7]; Dasgupta 2007 [8]; Theory 2013 [35]; De Tombe 2015 [9]; Brundtland Commission 1987 [5]; Weizsacker, Wijkman 2018 [39]; Zgurovsky and Statyukha 2010 [40]). Here we give only ideas on the construction of models and what can be obtained with the help of these models. At the same time, we will try to identify a special part of SD modeling that was least reflected in existing methods, concepts, models – namely, population properties, knowledge production, learning processes in a broad sense, a generation change. First, let us recall a more or less general idea of the three 'pillars' in the SD process (Fig. 6).

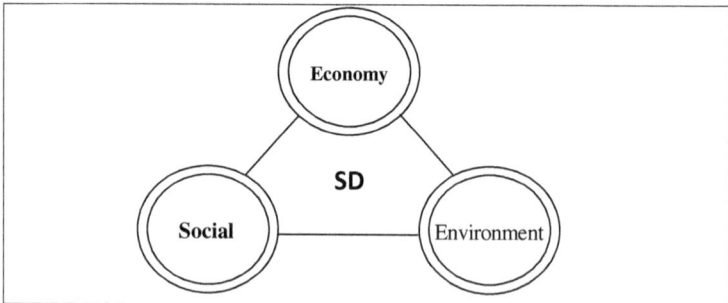

Fig. 6. Three 'pillars' SD

(Note that many SD indices are based exactly on such a partition). The model concepts of the "social" block are comparatively less developed (although there already exists a special discipline called "social informatics").

The most developed class of models is the block "Environment" – there are differential equations in partial derivatives (atmosphere, pollution, climate change), system dynamics, econometrics, stochastic equations, CA, etc.). The economy also has many good established models: models of micro- and macroeconomics, game theory, stochastic differential equations, econometrics, and, more recently, multi-agent systems.

The model concepts of the "social" block are comparatively less developed (although there already exists a special discipline called "social informatics." There are models in the psychology of the individual, game theory and multi-agent systems, partial differential equations (Kapitsa et al. 1997; Vorobiev et al. 1998), cognitive maps, but to the fullest extent The models with associative memory (Makarenko 1994, 1998, 2002, 2013) allow us to satisfy the requirements for the modeling of social systems.

There are models in the psychology of the individual, game theory and multiagent systems, partial differential equations (Kapitsa et al. 1997 [15]; Vorobiev et al. 1998 [36]), cognitive maps, but to the fullest extent the models with associative memory (Makarenko 1994 [20], 1998 [23], 2002 [18], 2013 [19]) allow us to satisfy the requirements for the modeling of social systems.

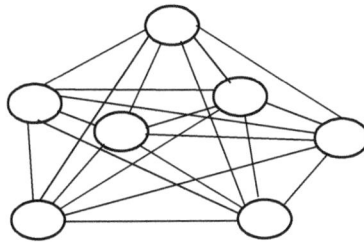

Fig. 7 Network structure

Note that this description is suitable both as a description of the external environment ("environment") of the element, and as a description of the internal individual's representation about the external world and the structure of existing knowledge (for example, semantic networks, cognitive maps, etc.). But in principle, phenomena from the blocks of ecology or economics also admit description and modeling using models with associative memory and network representation of the system. Sometimes it's quite simple and almost obvious, sometimes it's not obvious and very difficult. The network approach to various systems is being successfully developed in physics, sociology, psychology, biology, economics, etc. (Watts and Strogats 1998 [38]; Prigogine 2000 [28]; Wallerstein 1998 [37]). Therefore, in principle, even a complete general SD model can be written in the form of connected network structures and their dynamics in the class of dynamics with associative memory. That is, all the regularities described in (Makarenko 1994 [20], 1998 [23], 2002 [18], 2013

[19]) and which can be present in such models can in principle be inherent in the global SD model.

Therefore, in the integrated SD model and especially its use, you should use all the available arsenal of models, linking them, but in principle everything can be translated into a single language of network descriptions and dynamics in the associative memory class. Note also that the local SD process (in the sense described above), when the time of the task is relatively short, on which conditions (both natural and social) do not have time to change significantly, it seems that in principle it is possible to model fairly well the already known models in first of all, differential. However, long-term changes, especially taking into account a significant change in society and in knowledge, can most simply be modeled by models with associative memory.

First, consider the simplest illustrations (hypothetical examples) and consider how different SD components in them can look (while distracting from the details of the dynamics). We take the (hypothetical) systems with a phase space, a two-dimensional plane, and consider the case of classical stationary points of a two-dimensional saddle-point system.

Then the illustrations Fig. 8, 9 are proposed for the case when the dynamics are such that A_1 and A_2 attractors are points. However, one can imagine a situation (it is well known in the theory of neural networks) that limit cycles and dynamic chaos can act as attractors (Haykin 1994 [13]). Fig. 8, 9 present the case when we assume for simplicity that the landscape (the "energy" functional) remains unchanged.

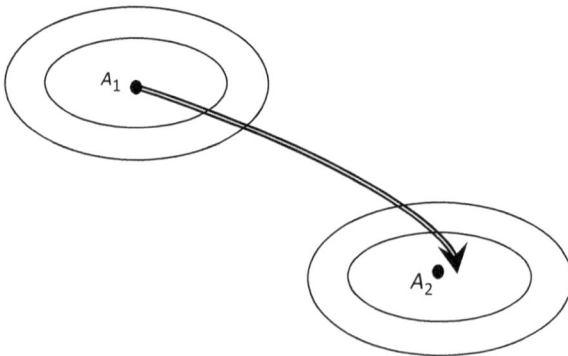

Fig. 8 .Managed of transition from an attractor A_1 to an attractor A_2

The next, more complicated, case interesting for SD can be considered such that the condition of transition from the region of attraction A_1 to the region of attraction A_2 is fulfilled.

In principle, even in the case of unrestricted, a rather complex management task already arises. If there are constraints, the task becomes even more complicated. In this case, the trajectory must go from one attractor to another (Fig. 8 is the case without restrictions, and in Fig. 9 limitations are shown).

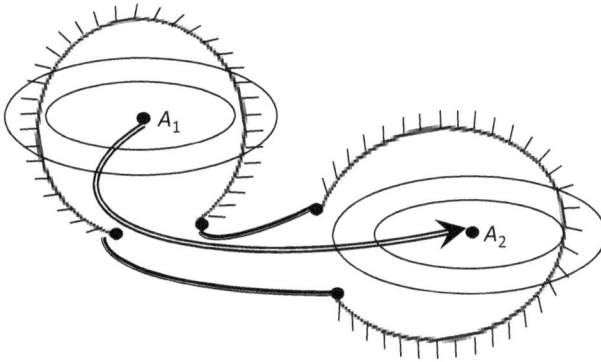

Fig. 9. An example (hypothetical) of considering an SD with two point attractors in the presence of constraints

If the attractor A_1 corresponds (conditionally) to one (the first) evolution interval $[0,T_1]$ of the system, and the attractor A_2 to the second evolution interval $[T_1,T_2]$ of the system, then we can say that if the trajectory from $[T_1,T_2]$ satisfies some SD criterion, then this case can be interpreted as taking into account the interests of subsequent generations.

We also point out a very important generalization of even such a simple model (recall that we assumed a fixed number of elements of their law of dynamics, connection and potential landscape, and there is only external control of the trajectory, which provides sustainability). Suppose that the potential landscape can change over time for external reasons (it is not yet important to discuss here for what reasons the landscape can change). Then the geometric structure of attractors and their domains of attraction, their number, stability properties, etc. can depend on the time and the SD problem in this case should be considered as the SD conditions for trajectories.

Up to now, explicitly or implicitly, we have discussed the situation when SD is assumed on the interval [0, T]. However, in reality, the very question of sustainability suggests that at present the state of affairs does not correspond to the sustainability plan, which is precisely the goal for the future. Therefore, in determining the SD, it is possible to require the fulfillment of a formal SD test from a certain instant of time on an interval $[T_*, T_2]$, or more generally on an interval $[T_*, +\infty)$. In this case, the SD criterion should be modified so that one SD criterion should be applied to the interval $[0, T_*]$, and other criterion (another SD criterion depending only on the future) on interval $[T_*, +\infty)$ or a minimum of costs on $[0, T_*]$. And, as indicated above, the trajectory can be not unique, and there can be a beam of trajectories.

A model example for considering such situations (and much more general) is the following situation. Suppose that on the interval $[0, T_1]$ the motion occurs conditionally in the neighborhood of the attractor A_1 and on the interval $[T_1, T_2]$ – in the neighborhood of the attractor A_2.

Let it be possible to somehow interpret the motion in the neighborhood of A_1 as non-sustainable, and in the neighborhood A_2 there is an opportunity for SD in the sense of the definitions we have introduced (do not forget that there can also be non-sustainable trajectories in the neighborhood of A_2).

This allows one to put a more general than pure SD task, namely the task of moving from non-sustainable development to sustainable one. Then it is possible to formally classify the transition tasks to SD: passing through barriers from the attractor to the attractor of the revolutionary type with the destruction of the landscape structure, and also gradual (evolutionary) with a slow (systematic) change in the landscape.

3.2 One approach to modeling external world representation in the proposed models

We call the set $Q^{(i)}(t)$ "the image of the real world" at a discrete time instant t. We also introduce $Q^{(i)}{}_{wish}(t)$ "the desired image of the world at moment t for the i-th individual" as a set of elemental states and desired connections for the first individual at a time.

$$Q^{(1)}_{\text{wish}}(t) = (\{s_i^{\text{wish}}(t)\},\ J_{ij}^{\text{wish}}(t)\}).$$

(5)

Then we assume that in the case of an isolated dynamic law, changes in the state of the first individual depend on the difference between the real and desirable image of the world:

$$D^{(i)}(t) = [[Q^{(i)}_{\text{wish}}(t) - Q^{(i)}(t)]]$$

(6)

Here $[[*]]$ is some norm. We present the prerequisites for introducing the difference (6) in model. Let us note that only the state of the real World is one for all personalities (in such models), but perceptions and "ideals" are different for different personalities. Fig. 10 presents "deformed" vision of the World by the individual. Exactly the same type of representation has the desired ("ideal") image of the World. Let us note that only the state of the real World is one for all personalities (in such models), but perceptions and "ideals" are different for different personalities.

If we want to represent the "inner" part of the dynamic law in the same way as the "outer" part in Section 2, then we can adopt a dynamic law for the first element of the form.

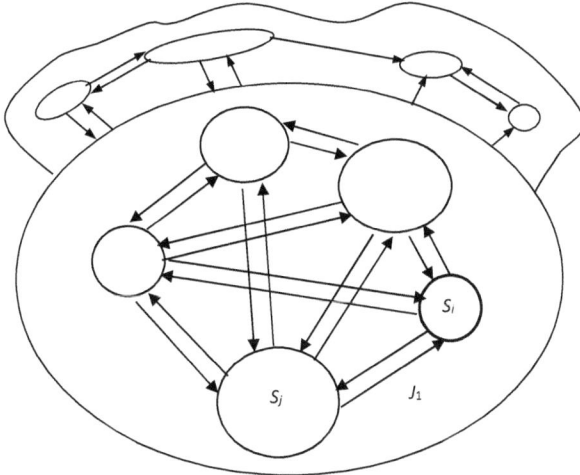

Fig. 10. The real state of the world and its internal representation (deformed) in the opinion of the individual

$$s_i(t+1) = F_i(h_i(t), D^{(i)}(t)).$$

Here $h_i(t)$ denotes the influence of the environment on i-th element, while $D^{(i)}(t)$ in formulas (5), (6) represents a part of the "internal representation". Function F takes into account both components of dynamic properties. The next step is to compare the desired image of the world with the actual images of the world at the moments of time $t,(t+1),(t+2),\ldots,(t+g(i))$, that are expected at these moments. Note that in the simplest case $g(i)=g(1)$. Parameters $\{g(i)\}$ determine the horizons of lead. The generalization of models in the case of taking into account the internal structures has the form

$$S_i(t+1)=F_i(h_i(t),D^{(i)}(t),D^{(i)}(t+1),\ldots D^{(i)}(t+g(i)));i=1,2,.$$

$$(7)$$

This system and its modifications can form a basis for investigating many problems with internal and external images of the world. Substitution of all components into the system leads to an equivalent system:

$$S_i(t+1)=G_i(\{s_i(t)\},\ldots\{s_i(t+g(i))\}R),$$

$$(8)$$

where R is the set of external (control, structural, environment) parameters. We must emphasize that the right-hand side of (8) depends on the future values of the state of the element. This form is contrasted with the form of equations with delay. It is very promising that the structure of system (8) coincides in structure with the anticipatory systems investigated by D. Dubois, 2001 [10, 11]. This implies a possible similarity in properties of the solutions. The most important property is presumable multivaluedness of solutions. The examples of equations with such behavior see in (Makarenko 2018 [24]).

REFERENCES

1. Aubin J.-P., Saint-Pierre P. An Introduction to Viability Theory and Management of Renewable Resourses. In: Decision-making and Risk Management in Sustainability Science, (eds. T. Kropp and J. Scheffran). N.Y.: Nova Science Publisher (2006)
2. Bak P., Sneppen K. Punctured Equilibrium and Criticality in a Simple model of evolution, Phys.Rev.Lett, 71, No. 24, P. 4083–4089 (1993)
3. Beradze M., Mnatsakanyan M., Makarenko A., Chikriy A. Optimal control in geopolitical problems, Vestn. Kharkiv Polytechnic Institute, No. 72, P. 8–12 (1999)
4. Van den Bergh J.C., Nijkamp P. Operationalizing Sustainable Development: Dynamic Economic Models, Ecological Economic, Vol. 4, P. 11–34 (1991)
5. Brundtland Commission. Report on the World Commission on Environment and Development. United Nations General Assembly, 96th Plenary Meeting 11 Dec. 1987. A/RES/42/187 (1987)
6. Chichilnisky G. An axiomatic approach to sustainable development, Social Chois and Welfare, Vol. 2, Issue 3, P. 231–257 (1996)
7. Daly H. From Uneconomic Growth to a Steady State Economy, Advanced in Ecological Economics, Chetlenham, UK (2014)
8. Dasgupta P. The idea of sustainable Development, Sustainability Science, Vol. 2, P. 5–11 (2007)
9. De Tombe D. Handling Societal Complexity. Springer-Verlag, Berlin-Heidelberg (2015)
10. Dubois D. Incursive and hyperincursive systems, fractal machine and anticipatory logic. Computing Anticipatory Systems: CASYS 2000 – Fourth International Conference. Published by the American Institute of Physics, AIP Conference Proceedings. 573, P. 437–451 (2001)
11. Dubois D. Theory of incursive synchronization and application to the anticipation of the chaotic epidemic, Int. J. of Comput Anticip. Syst. (Liege) , Vol. 10", P. 3–18 (2001)
12. Goals, Sustainable development goals, https://sustainabledevelopment.un.org/?menu=1300 (2015)
13. Haykin S. Neural Networks: Comprehensive Foundations, MacMillan: N.Y. (1994)
14. Hellman F., Shultz P., Grabow C., Heitzig J., Kunsths J. Survivability of Deterministic Dynamic Systems, Scientific Reports (Nature), Vol. 6: 29654 (2016)

15. Kapitsa S., Kurdyumov S., Malinetskiy G. Synergetics and forecasts of the future, Moscow, Nauka (1997)
16. Lefebvre V.A. Algebra of conscience. Dordrecht: Reidell (1982)
17. Levkov S., Makarenko A., Zelinsky V. Neuronet type models for stock market trading patterns, Proc. 5th Ukrainian Conference AUTOMATICA'98, Kiev, May, 1998, P. 162–166 (1998)
18. Makarenko A. Anticipating in the modeling of large social systems – neuronets with internal structure and multivaluedness, Int. J. of Computing Anticipatory Systems, 13, P. 77–92 (2002)
19. Makarenko A. Neuronet models of global processes with intellectual elements, International business: Innovation, Psychology, Economics, 4, No. 1(6), P. 65–83 (2013)
20. Makarenko A. About models of global socio-economic processes, Reports of the Ukrainian Academy of Sciences, No. 12, P. 85–87 (1994) [in Russian]
21. Makarenko A., Klestova Z. A new class of global models of associative memory type as a tool for considering global environmental change, Environmental Change, Adaptation, and Security, Ed. By S.C. Lonergan, NATO ASI Series, 2. Environment, Vol. 65, Kluwer Academic Publishers (1999)
22. Makarenko A. Global social conflicts and their models In: Confliktologikal expertaie: Theory and methodology. Vol. 1. Kiev: Conlictologis Association of Ukraine, P. 87–95 (1997) [in Russian]
23. Makarenko A. New Neuronet Models of Global Socio-Economical Processes // Gaming / Simulation for Policy Development and Organizational Change. J. Geurts, C. Joldersma, E. Roelofs eds, Tillburg: Tillburg University Press, P. 128–132 (1998)
24. Makarenko A. Multivaluedness Aspects in Self-Organization, Complexity and Computations Investigations by Strong Anticipation. Chapter in Book: Recent Advances in Nonlinear Dynamics and Synchronization. Eds. K. Kyamakya , W. Mathis, R. Stoop, J. Chedjou, Z. Li, Springer; Cham, P. 33–54 (2018)
25. Our Common Future, https://www.iisd.org/topic/sustainable-development (2018)
26. Paksoy T., Ozceylan E., Weber G.-W. A multi Objective Model for Optimization of a Green Supply Chain Network, Global Journal of Technology and Optimization, Vol. 2, P. 84–96 (2011)
27. Pezzey J. Sustainability constraints versus Intertemporal Concern, and Axioms Versus Data, Land Economics, Vol. 73, P. 448–466 (1997)

28. Prigogine I. The Networked Society, J. World-Syst. Res, 6, No. 3, P. 892–898 (2000)

29. Rand D.A., Wilson H.B. Evolutionary Catastrophes, Punctuated Equilibria and Gradualism in Ecosystem Evolution, Proc. Roy. Society London, Vol. 253, P. 131–141 (1993)

30. Rogers P., Jalal K.F., Boyd J.A. An Introduction to Sustainable Development, Routledge (2007)

31. Sheffran J., Brzoska M., Brauch H.-G., Link P., Schelling J. Climate Change, human Security and Violent conflict: Challenges for Societal Stability, Springer Science and Business Media, Vol. 8 (2012)

32. Scheffran J., Pickl S. Control and Game-theoretic Assessment of Climatchange: Options for Joint Implementations, Annals of Operational Research, Vol. 97, P. 203–212 (2000)

33. Soros G. Open society: reforming global capitalism, NY: Public Affairs (2000)

34. Sutton J.P., Beis J.S., Trainor L.E.H. Hierarchical model of memory and memory loss, Jour. of Phys. A: Math. Gen., 21, P. 4443–4454 (1988)

35. Theory and Implementation of Economic Models for Sustainability, Eds. J.C. van den Bergh, M.W. Hofkes, Springer (2013)

36. Vorobiev Yu.L., Malinetskiy G.G., Makhutov N.A. Theory of risk and security technology. Approach from positions of nonlinear dynamics, Proc. SICPRO'1998, Moscow: IPU, 2 p. (1998)

37. Wallerstein I. The Heritage of Sociology, The Promise of Social Science, Presidential Address, XIV-th World Congress of Sociology, Montreal, July 26, 1998, Part 2, http://fbc.binghampton.edu/iwprad2.htm (1998)

38. Watts D.J., Strogatz S. Collective dynamics of "small-world" networks, Nature, 393, P. 440–442 (1998)

39. Weizsacker E.U., Wijkman A. Come On! Capitalism, Short-termism, population and the Destruction of the Planet. N.Y.: Springer Science + Business Media, LLC (2018)

40. Zgurovsky M.Z., Statyukha G.A. Fundamentals of sustainable development of society, Part 1, Kiev: NTUU "KPI" (2010)

CHAPTER V

ANTICIPATIONS IN MODELS AND IN NATURE

1. The role of strong and weak anticipation in SD processes

We point out here some important problems of using the SD concept and considering the local and global aspects of SD. A useful tool in the practice of regional management is the use of mathematical modeling to predict the flow of processes in various fields: ecology, economics, social. Mathematical modeling in regional planning is used to predict possible scenarios for the evolution of real natural, technical, and social systems. Typically, real regional management experts view SD as a certain 'best' mode in the operation of a particular system. Often the consideration of the 'needs of the next generations' is neglected. Also, usually with local management, they do not consider the means and tasks for modeling the distant future. Note that a 'long-term' prediction is most often impossible primarily because of the initial complexity of such systems. In the second, the impossibility of forecasting a single path of development for large technical-economic-ecological systems is recognized by all. So for now, the arguments about the "further needs of the generations" are applicable rather when considering global theoretical problems.

But sustainable development processes can be treated adequately from the point of view of systems by antisipation (anticipation), especially with the "strong" and "weak" anticipation introduced by Daniel Dubois since the 1990s (Dubois 2001; Makarenko 2002; Makarenko 2013). Many formal definitions have been described in the literature (see for example (Makarenko 1994, 2013; Dubois 2001). Here we recall one of the definitions that are useful for understanding the role of antipathy in SD.

"Dubois (Dubois 2001, 2001a) shared a weak anticipation, that is, when systems use the model of themselves and the environment to calculate future states, and strong anticipation, that is, when the system uses itself to create its future states. In the latter case, the antipathy is no longer similar to the prediction ".

Therefore, 'local management' SD (using prediction) corresponds to a weak anticipation. But the situation with the global SD problem is completely different. Only the above formal definition of SD above (Chapter 1) Makes it possible to use the strong anticipation property for the global systems under consideration. That is, it is allowed to consider the future behavior of large social systems in the case of impossibility of prediction. Some possible confirmation of the anticipation property for social systems has been described earlier.

Also, many applications of such ideas (anticipation) for SD problems can be used for real system research and in management practice. Here we only need to emphasize the importance of sustainability (SD) education and the scientific system as one of the main tasks for SD of any large social system. For example, the possibility of sustainable development of the energy industry and the development of energy resources depends strongly on the development, first of all, of new knowledge about physical processes. For example, the development of nuclear power plants depends strongly on the development of nuclear physics.

Thus, the ideas described in this subsection support the possibilities for further development of the formal definition of sustainable development and allow us to formulate the SD problems on a rigorous basis. In the following subsections we will consider several such problems.

1.1 Anticipation and possible consequences in models

We recall very briefly the descriptions of the anticipation (Dubois 2001; Makarenko 1994, 2002, 2013 ; Dubois 2001).

A weak anticipation is when the system has a model for predicting future behavior. Strong antisipation is when the future state of the system is not known, but is taken into account to assess the transition at a given time.

The main essential new property in this case in the behavior of model solutions is the possibility of a multivalued solution (this set of possible values of the solution for certain instants of time exist under the unique initial conditions of the system (Makarenko 1994, 2002, 2013). This can be interpreted as the possibility of many development scenarios for real social systems.

The second key problem is connected with the fact that the real social system has a single realization of the historical path (the trajectory of the system actually being realized). That is, the social system as a whole makes a choice of its own trajectory at any time.

The local SD process is usually a process with a weak anticipation. Global SD processes are strongly anticipative. Consideration of scenarios and selection of a solution (scenario) can be considered on the basis of consideration of multivalued solutions and the choice of a single trajectory (Makarenko and

Klestova 1999; Makarenko 1997, 1998,: Beradze et al. 1999, Levkov et al. 1998). Below we give some geometrical illustrations of possible situations.

In Fig. 1 below illustrates the evolution of a system with a strong anticipation with time-limited resource constraints. New in comparison with conventional models is the case of the possibility of the existence of alternative scenarios (polysemy in solutions).

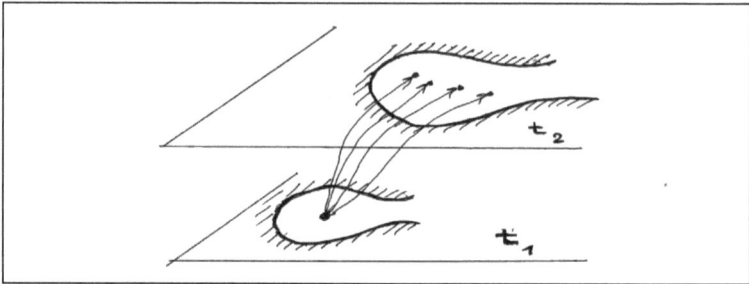

Fig. 1. Multiplicity of possible scenarios in a system with strong anticsipation

Fig. 2 corresponds to a much more complex (but also closer to reality) situation, where the limitations in the future change with time and depend on the possible evolution of the system. Moreover, in this case, the constraints themselves can acquire a many-valued form, which significantly complicates the mathematical formulation of the corresponding problems. Such a picture in principle just corresponds best to the situation of unknown future knowledge. We note that the restrictions in this case can be formalized as a mathematical object in various ways - as nonlinear equations, in classes of fuzzy sets or statistical distributions; other types of uncertainties; differential equations; variational inequalities, etc.

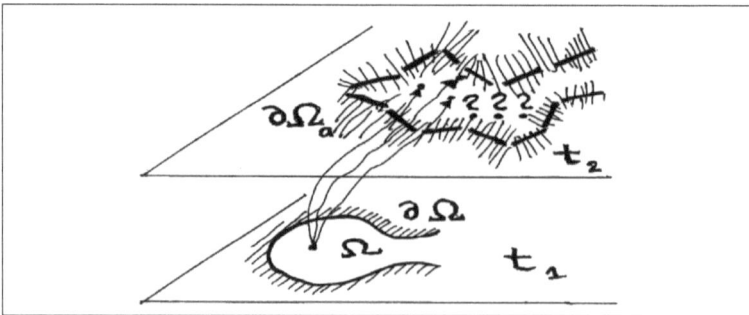

Unknown virtual anticipated restrictions in a system with strong anticipation

Further, when considering constraints unknown in time, other aspects should also be considered (for example, geometric or topological). Note that the above

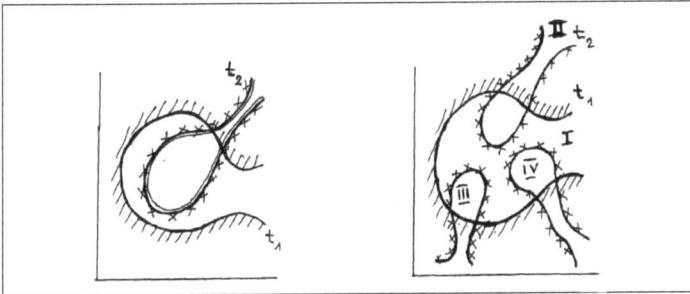

Fig. 3. Examples of the evolution of resource constraints. Left - "evolutionary", right -"fragmentation".

considerations are also new when considering and assessing risks in large socio-technical and economic systems. In this case, many possible problems arise-see, for example, Fig. 3 below.

2. Indices of sustainable (supported) development

Considerations of subsections 1-4 from Chapter IV can also help in solving another important problem in the supported development - namely, in the search for indices of sustainable development. Recently, many such indices have been proposed for different scales, different tasks and different organizations and institutions (UN Approach, World Bank indicators, government indices of different countries). But the general problem of indicators of the degree of

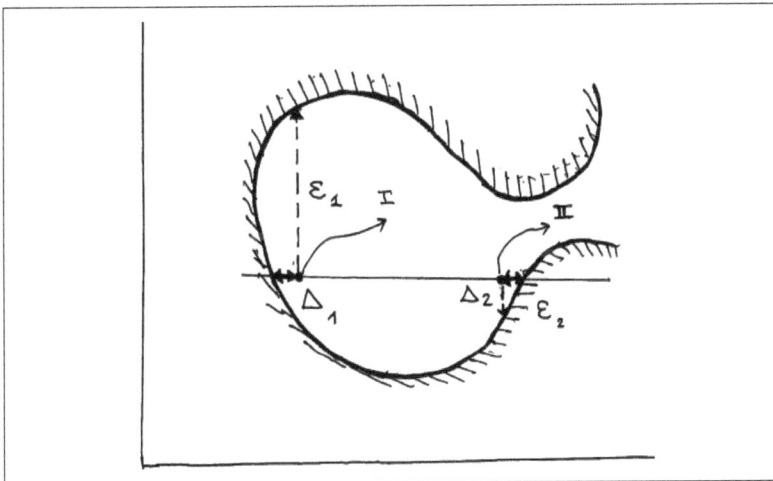

Fig. 4. An illustration of the case of different deviations for indices with respect to individual coordinates (ε_1 and ε_2) for two different points (Δ_1 and Δ_2) in the constraint area

support is open. This is partly due to the single-step nature of the indices used. According to the analysis of sustainable development, there is some hierarchy of the proposed indices depending on the selected process details in the system. The simplest case corresponds to a small number of essential parameters in the system. For example, the parameters can belong to some space X (often $X = R^N$, N is not a very large integer, usually less than 100). Then in the simplest case we can consider fixed constraints in the space X. We will give two-dimensional illustrations for illustration of some principal moments.

So, going back to the general case, we have $X = R^N$, $\Omega \subset X$, c_{ij}, where $\vec{s}(t)$ is the state vector of the system for which the supported development should be considered. It is important that not only the states of the system at the given moment t are important, but also the evolution of the system should be taken into account, since the dynamics of the trajectory of the system with respect to constraints $\vec{s}(t)$ (where $\partial\Omega$ there is a boundary of the domain of limitations Ω in question Ω) is important. We introduce the quantity

$$J(t) = J(\Delta(\vec{s}(\tau), \tau \in [t,T)) \Omega, \partial\Omega, X; T) \tag{1}$$

as an integral index (or vector of indices) of the degree of support of the moment t. In formula (1) $\Delta(\vec{s}(\tau), \tau \in [t,T))$ there is some integral estimate of the distance of the trajectory up to the constraint $\partial\Omega$ on some time interval $[t,T)$. Implicitly in this case, we assume that the trajectories $\vec{s}(t)$ of the system can be calculated using some models. The estimates $\Delta(s(t))$ can also include derivatives of time indices and other operators. That is, this way of calculating the stability indices corresponds to a weak antiposition. We note that in the special case $T = t$ we arrive at the case of existing support indices.

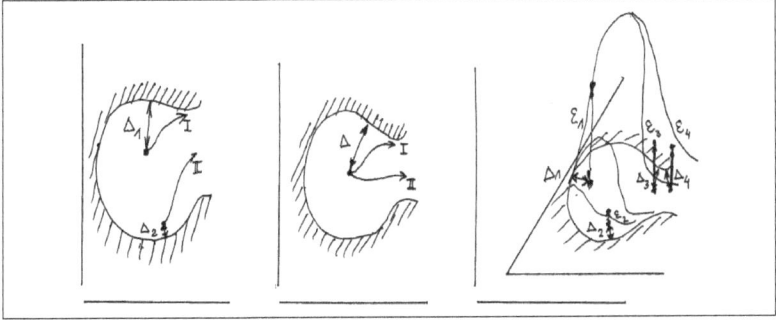

Fig. 5. Comparison of the trajectories coming from different points (on the left), different trajectories originating from one point (in the middle) and in the presence of the third (additional dimension (on the right)

The case of more complex systems requires a more developed definition of indicators (simply for a simplified case of fixed constraints) because of the large dimensions of real systems. Note that the case of time-varying constraints can be considered when calculating Δ with non-constant ones. $\partial \Omega \ (t)$

The second problem arising from the high dimensions of the system under consideration is more complex. Usually in the case of studies of sustainable development, only a small number of measurements are known (usually from some space R^{N_1}). In this case, we can divide all parameters N into two parts - N_1 measurable parameters (or visible parameters) and $N_2 = N - N_1$ - internal (invisible) parameters. In this case, formula (1) must be changed to the following formula

$$J(t) = J(\Delta_1(\vec{s}(\tau), \tau \in [t, T)); \Omega_1; \partial\Omega_1;$$
$$\Delta_2(\vec{s}(\tau), \tau \in [t, T)); \Omega_2; \partial\Omega_2; X; T) \qquad (2)$$

Where $\Delta_1(\vec{s}(\tau), \tau \in [t, T))$ there is an estimate of the distance from the constraints for the measured parameters and $\Delta_2(\vec{s}(\tau), \tau \in [t, T))$ is the estimate for the distance from the constraints for the internal parameters.

Therefore, the construction of such indices (the estimation of the possibility of supporting $J(t)$ in the case of weak anticipation is in principle known, but it can be technically complicated, especially in the search for adequate indices for real

71

data. Such a path for the computation of degree indices is most suitable for the case of 'local' control.

But much more interesting is the general case of sustained development, when it is necessary to take into account a strong anticipation (Dubois 2001, 2001a; Makarenko 2002). Here we recall one of the definitions that are useful for understanding the role of anticipation in SD.

"Dubois (Dubois 2001, 2001a). Formal constructions of support indexes above can easily be formally modified. But the meaning of such constructions and the results obtained can change fundamentally, mainly because of the main difference between weak and strong expectations. Note that according to the ideas on weak and strong expectations (Dubois 2001, 2001a; Makarenko 2002), in the case of strong expectation, the system creates itself. In this case, we can not predict the trajectories of the system, and the constraints depend on the evolution of the systems under consideration. Therefore, in this case, we can talk about 'antipaed' (future, born) constraints on a possible area of space for system variables. And then we can not calculate the distance from future unknown constraints. This leads to the need to study models with strong anticipation, their multivalued solutions and many-valued limitations. Each of the decision branches will have a different possible variety of constraints. Also, the average risk for different control values should be considered as an essential part of the stability indices. In this case, the definition of the index (indices) of sustainable development should be changed. For the simplest case this can be considered as follows

$$\tilde{J}(t) = J(\tilde{\Delta}\{\vec{s}(\tau)\}, \{\tilde{\Omega}(\tau)\}, \{\partial\tilde{\Omega}(\tau)\}, \tau \in [t,T)) \,, \tag{3}$$

Where $\{\vec{s}(t)\}$ is the possible set of trajectories of the system, ($\{\tilde{\Omega}(\tau)\}$, $\{\partial\tilde{\Omega}(\tau)\}, \tau \in [t,T))$ - the possible set of constraints, $\tilde{\Delta}$ - the distance between the set of possible trajectories and constraints. We note that in the case of systems with discrete time steps the set $(\{\tilde{\Omega}(\tau)\}, \tau \in [t,T))$ has, for example, the form

$$\{\tilde{\Omega}(\tau)\} = \{\Omega(t), \Omega(t+1), \Omega(t+2),...,\Omega(t+T)\} \,,$$

which is more suitable for the application of existing theories of strongly anticipative systems (Dubois 2001, 2001a; Makarenko 2002)..

That is, in the provided subsection, we formulated some considerations on the possibility of constructing an index of intelligent development. Further development of the theory and choice of adequate practical indices will depend on the use of various mathematical models of the system. Therefore, in the following sections, we briefly describe some facts about our models that are useful for considering sustainable development. It is interesting that such a global SD somehow echoes with the ideas of global theology.

Remark 1. Constraints can vary in time, be very complex, and for individual components there can be equations of different nature, which depend on the solutions themselves and on the interacting systems themselves. It is appropriate to use the concepts of synergetic: including the concepts of driven and leading parameters, bifurcations, SOK (self-organized criticality), dissipative structures, order parameters, fluctuations.

Remark 2. One can more or less adequately take into account the uncertainty in the local SD.

Remark 3. It is possible to take into account the aspects related to the presence of different generations (the conservation of resources for solving such problems can also be taken into account by setting the problems through different functionals related to SD, while for the next generations the uncertainty is qualitatively different, which can also be taken into account in the proposed scheme .

REFERENCES

1. Aubin J.-P., Saint-Pierre P. An Introduction to Viability Theory and Management of Renewable Resourses. In: Decision-making and Risk Management in Sustainability Science, (eds. T. Kropp and J. Scheffran). N.Y.: Nova Science Publisher (2006)
2. Bak P., Sneppen K. Punctured Equilibrium and Criticality in a Simple model of evolution, Phys.Rev.Lett, 71, No. 24, P. 4083–4089 (1993)
3. Beradze M., Mnatsakanyan M., Makarenko A., Chikriy A. Optimal control in geopolitical problems, Vestn. Kharkiv Polytechnic Institute, No. 72, P. 8–12 (1999)
4. Van den Bergh J.C., Nijkamp P. Operationalizing Sustainable Development: Dynamic Economic Models, Ecological Economic, Vol. 4, P. 11–34 (1991)
5. Brundtland Commission. Report on the World Commission on Environment and Development. United Nations General Assembly, 96th Plenary Meeting 11 Dec. 1987. A/RES/42/187 (1987)
6. Chichilnisky G. An axiomatic approach to sustainable development, Social Chois and Welfare, Vol. 2, Issue 3, P. 231–257 (1996)
7. Daly H. From Uneconomic Growth to a Steady State Economy, Advanced in Ecological Economics, Chetlenham, UK (2014)
8. Dasgupta P. The idea of sustainable Development, Sustainability Science, Vol. 2, P. 5–11 (2007)
9. De Tombe D. Handling Societal Complexity. Springer-Verlag, Berlin-Heidelberg (2015)
10. Dubois D. Incursive and hyperincursive systems, fractal machine and anticipatory logic. Computing Anticipatory Systems: CASYS 2000 – Fourth International Conference. Published by the American Institute of Physics, AIP Conference Proceedings. 573, P. 437–451 (2001)
11. Dubois D. Theory of incursive synchronization and application to the anticipation of the chaotic epidemic, Int. J. of Comput Anticip. Syst. (Liege) , Vol. 10", P. 3–18 (2001)
12. Goals, Sustainable development goals, https://sustainabledevelopment.un.org/?menu=1300 (2015)
13. Haykin S. Neural Networks: Comprehensive Foundations, MacMillan: N.Y. (1994)
14. Hellman F., Shultz P., Grabow C., Heitzig J., Kunsths J. Survivability of Deterministic Dynamic Systems, Scientific Reports (Nature), Vol. 6: 29654 (2016)

15. Kapitsa S., Kurdyumov S., Malinetskiy G. Synergetics and forecasts of the future, Moscow, Nauka (1997)
16. Lefebvre V.A. Algebra of conscience. Dordrecht: Reidell (1982)
17. Levkov S., Makarenko A., Zelinsky V. Neuronet type models for stock market trading patterns, Proc. 5th Ukrainian Conference AUTOMATICA'98, Kiev, May, 1998, P. 162–166 (1998)
18. Makarenko A. Anticipating in the modeling of large social systems – neuronets with internal structure and multivaluedness, Int. J. of Computing Anticipatory Systems, 13, P. 77–92 (2002)
19. Makarenko A. Neuronet models of global processes with intellectual elements, International business: Innovation, Psychology, Economics, 4, No. 1(6), P. 65–83 (2013)
20. Makarenko A. About models of global socio-economic processes, Reports of the Ukrainian Academy of Sciences, No. 12, P. 85–87 (1994) [in Russian]
21. Makarenko A., Klestova Z. A new class of global models of associative memory type as a tool for considering global environmental change, Environmental Change, Adaptation, and Security, Ed. By S.C. Lonergan, NATO ASI Series, 2. Environment, Vol. 65, Kluwer Academic Publishers (1999)
22. Makarenko A. Global social conflicts and their models In: Confliktologikal expertaie: Theory and methodology. Vol. 1. Kiev: Conlictologis Association of Ukraine, P. 87–95 (1997) [in Russian]
23. Makarenko A. New Neuronet Models of Global Socio-Economical Processes // Gaming / Simulation for Policy Development and Organizational Change. J. Geurts, C. Joldersma, E. Roelofs eds, Tillburg: Tillburg University Press, P. 128–132 (1998)
24. Makarenko A. Multivaluedness Aspects in Self-Organization, Complexity and Computations Investigations by Strong Anticipation. Chapter in Book: Recent Advances in Nonlinear Dynamics and Synchronization. Eds. K. Kyamakya , W. Mathis, R. Stoop, J. Chedjou, Z. Li, Springer; Cham, P. 33–54 (2018)
25. Our Common Future, https://www.iisd.org/topic/sustainable-development (2018)
26. Paksoy T., Ozceylan E., Weber G.-W. A multi Objective Model for Optimization of a Green Supply Chain Network, Global Journal of Technology and Optimization, Vol. 2, P. 84–96 (2011)
27. Pezzey J. Sustainability constraints versus Intertemporal Concern, and Axioms Versus Data, Land Economics, Vol. 73, P. 448–466 (1997)

28. Prigogine I. The Networked Society, J. World-Syst. Res, 6, No. 3, P. 892–898 (2000)

29. Rand D.A., Wilson H.B. Evolutionary Catastrophes, Punctuated Equilibria and Gradualism in Ecosystem Evolution, Proc. Roy. Society London, Vol. 253, P. 131–141 (1993)

30. Rogers P., Jalal K.F., Boyd J.A. An Introduction to Sustainable Development, Routledge (2007)

31. Sheffran J., Brzoska M., Brauch H.-G., Link P., Schelling J. Climate Change, human Security and Violent conflict: Challenges for Societal Stability, Springer Science and Business Media, Vol. 8 (2012)

32. Scheffran J., Pickl S. Control and Game-theoretic Assessment of Climat-change: Options for Joint Implementations, Annals of Operational Research, Vol. 97, P. 203–212 (2000)

33. Soros G. Open society: reforming global capitalism, NY: Public Affairs (2000)

34. Sutton J.P., Beis J.S., Trainor L.E.H. Hierarchical model of memory and memory loss, Jour. of Phys. A: Math. Gen., 21, P. 4443–4454 (1988)

35. Theory and Implementation of Economic Models for Sustainability, Eds. J.C. van den Bergh, M.W. Hofkes, Springer (2013)

36. Vorobiev Yu.L., Malinetskiy G.G., Makhutov N.A. Theory of risk and security technology. Approach from positions of nonlinear dynamics, Proc. SICPRO'1998, Moscow: IPU, 2 p. (1998)

37. Wallerstein I. The Heritage of Sociology, The Promise of Social Science, Presidential Address, XIV-th World Congress of Sociology, Montreal, July 26, 1998, Part 2, http://fbc.binghampton.edu/iwprad2.htm (1998)

38. Watts D.J., Strogatz S. Collective dynamics of "small-world" networks, Nature, 393, P. 440–442 (1998)

39. Weizsacker E.U., Wijkman A. Come On! Capitalism, Short-termism, population and the Destruction of the Planet. N.Y.: Springer Science + Business Media, LLC (2018)

40. Zgurovsky M.Z., Statyukha G.A. Fundamentals of sustainable development of society, Part 1, Kiev: NTUU "KPI" (2010)

CHAPTER VI

SHORT DESCRIPTION OF ASSOCIATIVE MEMORY APPROACH FOR SOME SOCIAL PROBLEMS

1. Introduction

First of all we stress some problems related to population participants at eGovernment: 1) formation of public opinion on some issue by electronic system; 2) voting on some question through eGovernment; 3) expanding of eGovernment system; 4) evaluation of power distribution between population and administration. Below we propose for illustration the development of methodology the first problem. Remark that in this paper we intend only to illustrate the background of methodology on the base of simplest examples.

1.1. General ideas

We present here briefly the core idea of the approach and the rough draft of the model that we are going to develop in the research. The proposed model does not pretend to be full and is intended only to demonstrate the basic ideas presented here.

As the first example we consider the simplified problem when all individual are involved in eGovernment system. Lets all individuals pose personal opinion through electronic networks and received some revised information through networks. Remark that the type and volume of information is different. The first is the case of fully open process when all individuals know the opinion of all involved participants. The second case is the backward distribution for all participants only the integral results (for example average opinion – say the percents of supporting individuals or the power of support of some issue).

In order to make easier understanding of the method and to simplify the initial formulas, we consider the idealized society. The opinion development consists of discrete steps, at which the actual exchange of opinion take place. Within each step we identify the sub steps, which describe the dynamic bidding and asking or decision-making processes for every individual. The society consists of N homogeneous participants (in future developments the homogeneous assumption obviously should be removed).

With every participant we associate the state variable $s_i \in S = \{0, \pm 1, \pm 2 \ldots, \pm M_i\}$,

where s_i represents the number of shares that participant i is planning to strength (if $s_i > 0$) or to weak (if $s_i < 0$) opinion, and M_i is the maximum allowed volume, which represents the power of opinion of participant i is able to accept.

With every pair of participants i and j we associate the variable $c_{ij} \in \mathbf{R}$ — the integral value of reputation that participant j has from the point of view of participant i. This value measures the degree of how well informed; participant j is in the eyes of the participant i. The large positive values of c_{ij} mean that, in the opinion of participant i, participant j is an informed (news, insider) participant, the values close to zero can mean that the participant j is an uninformed (noise, nice) or liquidity participant, while the negative values mean that the participant j is either insider who work against the information he has in order to hide himself, or a participant who is likely to be wrong in his judgment. The reputation variables c_{ij} form a matrix

$$C = \{c_{ij}\}_{i,j=1,...,N} \tag{1}$$

that we call the matrix of reputation. The approach c_{ij} valuation will be discussed later at the end of this section.

As one of the basic characteristics of the system we introduce the concept of a vector field of influence

$$F = \{f_i\}_{i=1,...,N} : f_i = \sum_j c_{ij} \frac{s_j}{M_j}, \quad c_{ii} = 0 \tag{2}$$

where f_i means the integral influence of opinions of all other participants on i participant. The intuition behind this formula is the following. The ratio $\frac{s_j}{M_j}$ represents the opinion intentions of participant j at the current step. It shows the number of opinion participant j is planning to support or reject as a percentage of what his actual power is. The product $c_{ij} \times \frac{s_j}{M_j}$ is the information about intentions of participant j filtered through the matrix of reputation. Thus, the sum (2) represents all the available to participant i information about the actions of other participants, and since it is filtered through the matrix of reputation, it is meaningful and trustworthy to him. We would like to note here, that all the other information, participant i might have, is already incorporated in his initial intensions s_i.

Obviously, the best strategy for rational individual will be to adjust his own initial intentions to the filtered information about others. Speaking formally, we say that every participant is associated with the information utility function, which he is trying to maximize during the decision-making process. It is done by correlating the decision of individual i with the corresponding value of the field of influence f_i.

Thus, we may formulate the evolution equation describing the opinion dynamics (of course it is the simplest possible example of dynamics):

$$s_i(t+1) =$$

$$= \begin{cases} s_i + 1, & \text{if } f_i(t) > 0 \text{ and } s_i(t) < M_i, \\ s_i - 1, & \text{if } f_i(t) < 0 \text{ and } s_i(t) > -M_i, \\ s_i & \text{otherwise} \end{cases} \quad (3)$$

The initial conditions for this dynamic equation are the intentions of each individual to support opinion at the beginning of the opinion forming step. They are formed under the influence of the sources outside the system, and represent the participant's forecast of how well the particular opinion distribution will be doing.

Given the initial conditions for s_i and known values of influence matrix, we may calculate the dynamics of the opinion patterns. Such dynamics is expected to be beneficial for each participant, since it leads to the maximal utilization of the filtered, and therefore useful, information available to him.

Obviously, the system consists of protagonists with different and frequently antagonistic goals. Thus, the actions beneficial for a particular participant do not necessarily benefit the others. Moreover, each participant acts from his own interests and generally, if somebody wins, someone loses. However, all these egoistic individuals comprise the system we consider. Therefore, from the system point of view the question is, whether the defined above dynamics of every participant leads to a meaningful evolution of the whole system, or is this just a disordered, chaotic motion? The answer can be found using the analogy with the physical systems.

As the variable summarizing the evolution of the system, we introduce the concept of 'energy' E, which characterizes the impact all the participants have had on each other in making their supporting/rejection decisions:

$$E = -\sum_i f_i s_i$$

Thus, at any given point in time, 'energy' E characterizes the state of the society. Naturally, we are interested in the evolution of the opinion patterns leading to a state that has the property of stability. By analogy with the physical systems, we will call the state of the system stable if the 'energy' E has a local minimum in this point. As we will see, the system will tend to minimize its energy during the evolution process. To show this, we will first formulate and prove the following statement.

Statement 1. Under the law of evolution (3) the system evolves to a local minimum of energy E.

After energy reaches the local minimum, due to (A1) any change of the state of the system will increase the energy, which is impossible because of (A2). Thus, $s_i(t+1) = s_i(t) \ \forall i$, and the system will retain its stable state until some external forces are applied. Such stable state can be thought as equilibrium, at which opinion pattern takes place. It simply means that all the participants have reached their decisions having maximized their own information utility functions. Since we are assuming that all the external information the participants might have is represented by their initial intentions, evolution occurs. Thus, maximization of individuals' information utility functions leads to the minimum of energy of the system and, therefore, to its coordinated movement during the decision-making step.

The next evolution step begins with the new initial conditions, which contain the new information participants have been able to obtain.

The reputation matrix in the described above model remains invariable during the supporting/rejection or decision-making steps. Obviously, it should change at each evolution step, since participants analyze their own performance as well as the performance of other participants and society as a whole. Therefore, each individual might assign different coefficients to the corresponding elements of the matrix of reputation, which will be enforced at the next evolution step.

Thus, the reputation matrix plays one of the major roles in the proposed model, and the applicability of the model depends, to a great extent, on the correctness and accuracy of the reputation coefficients. The numeric values for the entries of the matrix of reputation are not readily available. However, one of the advantages of the given approach is that it uses already proved and experimentally tested algorithms for the identification of the matrix C via the prior observations of the opinion patterns. This algorithm has the form of the well-known rule from the pattern recognition theory of associative memory models [7]. Its brief idea can be outlined as follows.

Suppose we have recorded information about opinion patterns Z_k, $k=1,..,K$, where $Z_k = \{s_i\}$ at the time moment k, K is the number of observations, $i=1,...,N$, N — number of participants. Then the matrix of reputation C can be evaluated as

$$C=\{c_{ij}\}, \quad c_{ij} = \sum_k \frac{s_{ik}}{M_i} \times \frac{s_{jk}}{M_j}, \quad c_{ii} = 0 \tag{4}$$

Of course such model correspond more to the case of opinion formation in parliaments, administrative councils, and cyberspace networks. But a lot of improvements of model can be proposed. Here we describe some of most evident.

Anyway more realistic is situation that only $F(\%)$ of population is involved in egovernance processes. Then the frames of the model are the same but for all population only opinions of N_e e-participants are known. This allows further developments. At first the opinion of this N_e participants serves as the information for other part on society by mass-media, social relations etc. Such information serves also as some kind of social questionnaires (with the same difficulties and problems). As such the date of e-participants opinion may serve as the database for other models and approaches. At second the changes in reputations $C = \{c_{ij}\}$ can be introduced. Such changes in reputations may have different reasons – internal and external. Internal changes have internal process of evolution as the source. External changes may have the mass-media influence, straggle of political parties, and education system as the main reasons. Remark that special dynamical equations may be derived for evolution of $C = \{c_{ij}\}$ during time flow [7].

Presumable variety of matrix of reputation properties may follow to a lot of different effects (which we cannot describe here because the lack of space). We only remark here the possibility of periodic solutions for slightly non-symmetrical matrix of reputation and chaotic behavior of public opinion in the case of sufficiently non-symmetric reputation matrix. Also the abrupt transition between quasi-stable stats of opinion during time in case of non-constant matrix of reputation $C=\{c_{ij}\}$.

2. Accounting the internal structures of e-Government participants

The next step in development of proposed models is to account the internal structure of participants (we named such participants as 'intellectual').
Let us consider the idealized system as the collection of N intellectual participants. We will consider the process with discrete time steps. Each participant should to do decision (change of state) at each time step in dependence of all participants' states [20].

Participant's state is described by the variable $S_i(t) \in S=\{0,\pm1,\pm2,..,\pm M_i\}$, which corresponds to the amount of the recourse (opinion, information, materials and so on), which may be gain (if $S_i(t)<0$) or collect (if $S_i(t)>0$) by i individual (participant). Here M_i is the maximal volume of its resource (its potential). Interaction of individuals in organization is described by influence matrix $C=\{c_{ij}\}$, $j=1,...,N$, $c_{ij} \in [0,1]$ where c_{ij} — influence coefficient of j individual on i. The influence matrix C may reflect the authority power in organization. In simplest model we take $C_{ij}=0$, $i=1,...,N$.

So the collection $Q^R(t)=\left(\{S_l^R(t)\},\{C_{lj}^R\}\right)$, $i,j=1,...,N$ represents the real state at moment t. Let us consider also $Q^i(t)=\left(\{S_l^i(t)\},\{C_{lj}^i\}\right)$, $i,j,l=1,...,N$ as ideal pattern of situation from the i participant point of view. Then we can calculate the difference between real and ideal patterns of situation:

$$D_i(t)=\left\|Q^i(t)-Q^R(t)\right\| \qquad (5)$$

We suppose that the dynamics of i participant depends on the difference $D_i(t)$ and on the mean influence field by other participants. We accept the influence field $G(t)=\{g_i(t)\}$, $i=1,...,N$ as:

$$g_i(t) = \sum_{j=1}^{N} C_{ij}^R \frac{S_j^R(t)}{M_j} \qquad (6)$$

The term $\dfrac{S_j^R(t)}{M_j}$ in (6) corresponds to the activity of j participant at the

moment t. The term $C_{ij}^R \dfrac{S_j^R(t)}{M_j}$ corresponds to activity with reputation

accounting. In general case the dynamical law for participant takes the form (F some law for participant's reaction, named frequently activation function):

$$S_i^R(t+1) = F(v_i(t)) \qquad (7)$$

where the argument $v_i(t)$ may takes the form:

a) Multiplicative

$$v_i(t) = \alpha(D_i(t))g_i(t) \qquad (8)$$

where for example $\alpha(D_i(t)) = e^{-kD_i(t)}$. In simplest evident variant we may take:

$$D_i(t) = \sum_{j=1}^{N} \left| S_j^i(t) - S_j^R(t) \right| \qquad (9)$$

b) additive $v_i(t) = g_i(t) + f_i(D_i(t))$, where $f_i(D_i(t))$ — some influence function. The simplest example is:

$$f(D_i(t)) = \sum_{j=1}^{N} C_{ij}^R \frac{(S_j^R S_j^i)}{M_j} \qquad (10)$$

In this model vector $v_i(t)$ represent the understanding by i participant on the tendencies in system: If $v_i(t) > 0$, then the tendency is to increase the recourse, if $v_i(t) \approx 0$, then the stability is the main tendency, if $v_i(t) < 0$, then the tendency is to reduce the resources.

One of the most usable forms of activation function F in such type models are:

$$S_i^R(t+1) =$$

$$\begin{cases} S_i^R(t)+1 & \text{if } v_i(t) > \dfrac{\|G(t)\|\|S_i^R\|}{M_i} \text{ and } S_i^R(t) < M_i, \\[4mm] S_i^R(t)-1 & \text{if } v_i(t) > \dfrac{\|G(t)\|\|S_i^R\|}{M_i} \text{ and } S_i^R(t) > -M_i, \\[4mm] 0 & \text{othervise} \end{cases} \qquad (11)$$

Where

$$\|G(t)\| = \frac{\sqrt{\sum\limits_{i=1}^{N} g_i^2(t)}}{N} \qquad (12)$$

Remark that very interesting development of proposed models consist in introduction time dependence of connections by some dynamical laws. Of course the models described here correspond to the constant bonds.

Thus in proposed section we consider the approach for system analysis and modeling which implement some properties of real society and eGovernment. The main distinctive features are the accounting of internal properties of participants. As the authors envisage, the modeling principles, described in section 3 can lead to the formulation and solution of the following problems:

1. Development of models of opinion patterns for the specific real problems.

2. Investigation of the control and security problems of eGovernment on the base of proposed approach.

3. Introducing and investigation different indexes of eGovernment operating, especially of power of e-participants community.

4. Numerical simulation of specific local eGovernment problems.

5. Analysis of the eGovernment spreading in society on the base of proposed methodology.

6. Forming proposition for building general tasks computing systems of investigation and managing eGovernment with accounting all aspects remarked above.

7. Proposed approach allows re-formulate the problems of cyber security of networks and more generally security of society.

REFERENCES

1. Aubin J.-P., Saint-Pierre P. An Introduction to Viability Theory and Management of Renewable Resourses. In: Decision-making and Risk Management in Sustainability Science, (eds. T. Kropp and J. Scheffran). N.Y.: Nova Science Publisher (2006)
2. Bak P., Sneppen K. Punctured Equilibrium and Criticality in a Simple model of evolution, Phys.Rev.Lett, 71, No. 24, P. 4083–4089 (1993)
3. Beradze M., Mnatsakanyan M., Makarenko A., Chikriy A. Optimal control in geopolitical problems, Vestn. Kharkiv Polytechnic Institute, No. 72, P. 8–12 (1999)
4. Van den Bergh J.C., Nijkamp P. Operationalizing Sustainable Development: Dynamic Economic Models, Ecological Economic, Vol. 4, P. 11–34 (1991)
5. Brundtland Commission. Report on the World Commission on Environment and Development. United Nations General Assembly, 96th Plenary Meeting 11 Dec. 1987. A/RES/42/187 (1987)
6. Chichilnisky G. An axiomatic approach to sustainable development, Social Chois and Welfare, Vol. 2, Issue 3, P. 231–257 (1996)
7. Daly H. From Uneconomic Growth to a Steady State Economy, Advanced in Ecological Economics, Chetlenham, UK (2014)
8. Dasgupta P. The idea of sustainable Development, Sustainability Science, Vol. 2, P. 5–11 (2007)
9. De Tombe D. Handling Societal Complexity. Springer-Verlag, Berlin-Heidelberg (2015)
10. Dubois D. Incursive and hyperincursive systems, fractal machine and anticipatory logic. Computing Anticipatory Systems: CASYS 2000 – Fourth International Conference. Published by the American Institute of Physics, AIP Conference Proceedings. 573, P. 437–451 (2001)
11. Dubois D. Theory of incursive synchronization and application to the anticipation of the chaotic epidemic, Int. J. of Comput Anticip. Syst. (Liege) , Vol. 10", P. 3–18 (2001)
12. Goals, Sustainable development goals, https://sustainabledevelopment.un.org/?menu=1300 (2015)
13. Haykin S. Neural Networks: Comprehensive Foundations, MacMillan: N.Y. (1994)
14. Hellman F., Shultz P., Grabow C., Heitzig J., Kunsths J. Survivability of Deterministic Dynamic Systems, Scientific Reports (Nature), Vol. 6: 29654 (2016)

15. Kapitsa S., Kurdyumov S., Malinetskiy G. Synergetics and forecasts of the future, Moscow, Nauka (1997)
16. Lefebvre V.A. Algebra of conscience. Dordrecht: Reidell (1982)
17. Levkov S., Makarenko A., Zelinsky V. Neuronet type models for stock market trading patterns, Proc. 5th Ukrainian Conference AUTOMATICA'98, Kiev, May, 1998, P. 162–166 (1998)
18. Makarenko A. Anticipating in the modeling of large social systems – neuronets with internal structure and multivaluedness, Int. J. of Computing Anticipatory Systems, 13, P. 77–92 (2002)
19. Makarenko A. Neuronet models of global processes with intellectual elements, International business: Innovation, Psychology, Economics, 4, No. 1(6), P. 65–83 (2013)
20. Makarenko A. About models of global socio-economic processes, Reports of the Ukrainian Academy of Sciences, No. 12, P. 85–87 (1994) [in Russian]
21. Makarenko A., Klestova Z. A new class of global models of associative memory type as a tool for considering global environmental change, Environmental Change, Adaptation, and Security, Ed. By S.C. Lonergan, NATO ASI Series, 2. Environment, Vol. 65, Kluwer Academic Publishers (1999)
22. Makarenko A. Global social conflicts and their models In: Confliktologikal expertaie: Theory and methodology. Vol. 1. Kiev: Conlictologis Association of Ukraine, P. 87–95 (1997) [in Russian]
23. Makarenko A. New Neuronet Models of Global Socio-Economical Processes // Gaming / Simulation for Policy Development and Organizational Change. J. Geurts, C. Joldersma, E. Roelofs eds, Tillburg: Tillburg University Press, P. 128–132 (1998)
24. Makarenko A. Multivaluedness Aspects in Self-Organization, Complexity and Computations Investigations by Strong Anticipation. Chapter in Book: Recent Advances in Nonlinear Dynamics and Synchronization. Eds. K. Kyamakya , W. Mathis, R. Stoop, J. Chedjou, Z. Li, Springer; Cham, P. 33–54 (2018)
25. Our Common Future, https://www.iisd.org/topic/sustainable-development (2018)
26. Paksoy T., Ozceylan E., Weber G.-W. A multi Objective Model for Optimization of a Green Supply Chain Network, Global Journal of Technology and Optimization, Vol. 2, P. 84–96 (2011)
27. Pezzey J. Sustainability constraints versus Intertemporal Concern, and Axioms Versus Data, Land Economics, Vol. 73, P. 448–466 (1997)

28. Prigogine I. The Networked Society, J. World-Syst. Res, 6, No. 3, P. 892–898 (2000)

29. Rand D.A., Wilson H.B. Evolutionary Catastrophes, Punctuated Equilibria and Gradualism in Ecosystem Evolution, Proc. Roy. Society London, Vol. 253, P. 131–141 (1993)

30. Rogers P., Jalal K.F., Boyd J.A. An Introduction to Sustainable Development, Routledge (2007)

31. Sheffran J., Brzoska M., Brauch H.-G., Link P., Schelling J. Climate Change, human Security and Violent conflict: Challenges for Societal Stability, Springer Science and Business Media, Vol. 8 (2012)

32. Scheffran J., Pickl S. Control and Game-theoretic Assessment of Climat-change: Options for Joint Implementations, Annals of Operational Research, Vol. 97, P. 203–212 (2000)

33. Soros G. Open society: reforming global capitalism, NY: Public Affairs (2000)

34. Sutton J.P., Beis J.S., Trainor L.E.H. Hierarchical model of memory and memory loss, Jour. of Phys. A: Math. Gen., 21, P. 4443–4454 (1988)

35. Theory and Implementation of Economic Models for Sustainability, Eds. J.C. van den Bergh, M.W. Hofkes, Springer (2013)

36. Vorobiev Yu.L., Malinetskiy G.G., Makhutov N.A. Theory of risk and security technology. Approach from positions of nonlinear dynamics, Proc. SICPRO'1998, Moscow: IPU, 2 p. (1998)

37. Wallerstein I. The Heritage of Sociology, The Promise of Social Science, Presidential Address, XIV-th World Congress of Sociology, Montreal, July 26, 1998, Part 2, http://fbc.binghampton.edu/iwprad2.htm (1998)

38. Watts D.J., Strogatz S. Collective dynamics of "small-world" networks, Nature, 393, P. 440–442 (1998)

39. Weizsacker E.U., Wijkman A. Come On! Capitalism, Short-termism, population and the Destruction of the Planet. N.Y.: Springer Science + Business Media, LLC (2018)

40. Zgurovsky M.Z., Statyukha G.A. Fundamentals of sustainable development of society, Part 1, Kiev: NTUU "KPI" (2010).

CHAPTER VII

TOWARD THE MENTALITY ACCOUNTING IN SOCIAL SYSTEMS MODELING

The purpose of the chapter. So far, studies of the influence of the mentality of individuals on the processes in society have been conducted to a large extent by methods of humanities, that is, intuitively and qualitatively. At the same time, it is well known that the mainstream of development of various sciences is the increasing use of methods of exact sciences, especially mathematics and physics. It should be noted that the author suggests the aspects of mathematical modeling of society, which allow to formalizetion and including the question of mentality and conduct modeling, including the formulation of real management plans.

In the Chapter III we had proposed the verbal description of some related with the mentality issues. Here we pose some formalization of related topics. We start here from some remembering of description from Chapters IV-VI, but then we give up some new aspects of formalization.

1. Towards mentality accountin in models

The mentality accounting requires considerations internal structures and incorporating them in global hierarchical models. There are many approaches for mentality accounting (see review of some aspects in [1-3]). The most natural way for implementing this task is to consider as model for internal structure also neuronet models. Remember that originally neuronet models were introduced in the investigation of brain. Firstly we should change the basic laws of models for the goal of mentality accounting. On phenomenological level it may be implemented by introducing subdivision of elements variable which describe the state of each of each of the elements on external (externally visible

variables) $Q_{i\,ext}$ and internal (mental) $Q_{i\,int}$ variables of ith element,

where N - number of elements and establishing laws for two blocks of parameters.

Here we for simplicity consider the description of element's variables as vectors. But in more complex cases it may be patterns, mathematical structures, hierarhies of variables. In proposals below we should also use the improvements of dynamical laws for each of elements. Following the approaches for neural network models the ith element has output and input variables and some dynamical laws for solution calculations. In general case external (visible) variables of other elements may serve as the input parameters. We mark such external outputs for i^{th} as vector $\vec{X}^i_{ext}$. An example is the economic variables. But sometimes an internal variables also may serve as the output. Mark such variables as vector $\vec{X}^i_{int}$. An examples are stereotypes of individuals for decision-making. We should also introduce the dynamical laws for values of each of outputs $\vec{Y}^i_{ext}$ and $\vec{Y}^i_{int}$, $i = 1,2,...,N$:

$$\vec{Y}^i_{ext} = \vec{f}_{ext}(\vec{X}^i_{ext}, \vec{X}^i_{int}, \vec{P}^i_{ext}, \vec{E}^i_{ext})$$

(1)

$$\vec{Y}^i_{int} = \vec{f}_{int}(\vec{X}^i_{ext}, \vec{X}^i_{int}, \vec{P}^i_{int}, \vec{E}^i_{int})$$

(2)

where $\vec{f}^i_{ext}, \vec{f}^i_{int}$ are the dynamical functions for external and internal output and input variables. $\vec{P}_{ext}, \vec{P}_{int}, \vec{E}_{ext}\vec{E}_{int}$ are some parameters and biases for i^{th} element. Remark that dynamical laws may take the forms useful for case of continual time or discrete time. The functions $\vec{f}^i_{ext}, \vec{f}^i_{int}$ may have absolutely different forms. For example equations for external variables may have neuronet form with ordinary differential equations for internal variables. But one of the most prospective ways for mentality account lies in searching equation (1), (2) also in neuronet class. Here proposed to introduce the intrinsic mental models of World in elements, which represent the individuals or decision-making organisations with human participation. The simplest way consists in representing image of World in the individual's brain or in model as collection of elements and bonds between elements. In such World pattern there exist place for representing individual himself with personal beliefs, skills, knowledge, preferences. The mental structures on other individuals are also represented.

One approach to modeling mentality. Remembering some issues from the subsection from Chapter V conserning description of internal properties of individuals. At first we should take into account different representation of word. Namely we take into account 3 aspects (three images of the world) related

89

to real world. The first image is the precise image (representation, knowledge on the real world) of real world. Such image exists in principle but nobody knows precisely such image. The second image of the world is knowledge of the individual about real state of the world in the internal representation of each of

i^{th} , i=1,2,...,N individuals (N is the number of elements of the society). Such representations may be different for different individuals. The third image of the world is "ideal" (desired) image of the world (including internal states of individual) in the internal representation of each of the individuals. Such "ideal" images also may be different for each of N individuals. It is very interesting that this 3 images of the world may be related to the concept of 3 worlds by K. Popper.

If we want to represent the "inner" part of the dynamic law in the same way as the "outer" part in Section 3, then we can adopt a dynamic law.

Then the laws for element evolution should depend on such representation. Formally we can introduce projection operators PR for representing image of outer World in the brain:

$$PR_i : W_{ext} = (\{\vec{X}_{ext}\}\{\vec{X}_{int}\}\{\vec{f}_{ext}\}\{\vec{f}_{int}\}\{J^{ext}_{ij}\}\vec{P},\vec{E}) \Rightarrow$$
$$\Rightarrow W_{int} = (\{\vec{X}^{int}_{ext}\}\{\vec{X}^{int}_{int}\},$$
$$\{\vec{f}^{int}_{ext}\}\{\vec{f}^{int}_{int}\}\{J^{int}_{ij}\},\vec{P}^{int},\vec{E}^{int}) \tag{3}$$

where the last index i in right hand of (5) indicate that variables is the internal representation of original parameters in i^{th} element. It is very important that each individual has own personal image of the World. Remark that the action of operator PR_i may be subdivides on the many local projection operators.

The equation (3) may be replaced by more complicated by inserting self-representation of him in right hand of (3). This may lead to equation of type

$$PR_i(recursive) : W_{ext} \Rightarrow W_{int}(recursive) \tag{4}$$

Equation (4) remember the equation (3) but right hand $W_{int}(recursive)$ now depends on self- representing by individual. Of course there may exist recursion with many levels of recursion as in the theory of reflexive systems by N.Luhman, D.Soros, S.Lefever and so on.

2. The models with evolutionary structure

In previous subsections we proposed some general considerations allowing mentality aspects accounting. Such aspects should be implemented in mathematical modeling. But full general model of society may be very complicated. For example it is well known in psychology that each individual has about 30000 different mental plans (different internal aspects, cognitive, behavioral etc.). It is impossible now to take into account all this aspects. So it is necessary to take more simple models with small number of mental plans. Just the models with accounting single aspects are very complex and interesting. The simplex case is in accounting of each individuals (elements) states. Such models directly related to the classical Hopfield neural network models. More interesting case corresponds to accounting two variables as the description of elements one eternally visible and one internal. The particularly interesting case is the case of different rate of such variables change.

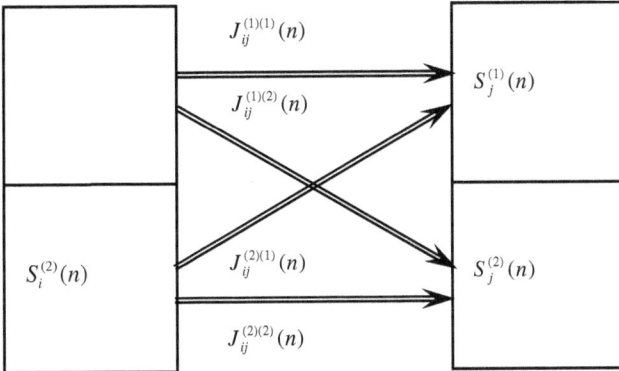

Fig. 1. Subdivision of variables on external/internal and slow/fast.

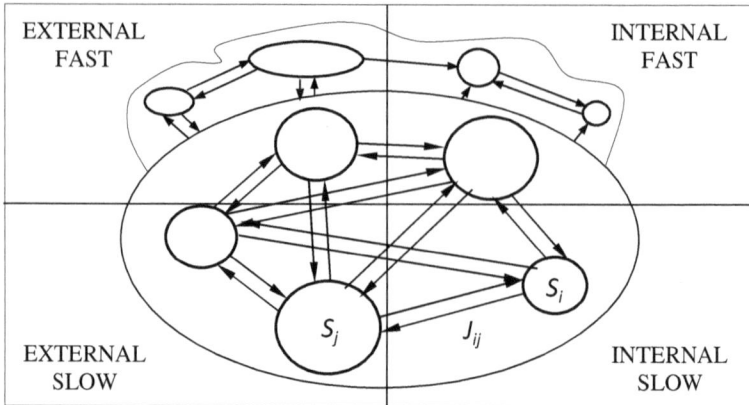

Fig. 2 Relationship of two two-state elements (i and j) at moment n, (1), (2) – index for slow and fast variables

Also for this paper approach and models very important are bounds beetwin different types of variables (external and internal). Remark that such bounds can changes with time and some external bias. Below we give for illustration the description of one of the simple models of such kind with two variables for each of elements.

New aspects in proposed models appear with taking into account the variable structure of models. The simplest variant includes allowing bonds dependence on time. Many variants of time dependence accounting in neuronal network architecture exist since the works by Hebb, McCallok and Pitts, T.Kohonenn , T.Hopfield and others. One simple example of proposed by author models with continuous time is (the indexes f correspond to 'fast' variables and parameters and indexes s correspond to 'slow' variables and parameters'):

$$
\begin{cases}
C^f_j \dfrac{dv^f_j(t)}{dt} = -\dfrac{v^f_j(t)}{R^f_j} + \\[2mm]
f^{ff} \left(\displaystyle\sum_{i=1}^{N} w^f_{ji}(t)\,\varphi^f_i(v^f_i(t)) \right) + \\[2mm]
f^{fs} \left(\displaystyle\sum_{i=1}^{N} w^s_{ji}(t)\,\varphi^s_i(v^s_i(t)) \right) + \\[2mm]
I^f_j + I^{fs}_j,
\end{cases}
$$

(5)-(8)

92

$$\begin{cases} C^s{}_j \dfrac{dv^s{}_j(t)}{dt} = - \dfrac{v^s{}_j(t)}{R^s{}_j} + \\[2mm] f^{ss}\left(\displaystyle\sum_{i=1}^{N} w^s{}_{ji}(t)\,\varphi^s{}_i(v^s{}_i(t))\right) + \\[2mm] f^{sf}\left(\displaystyle\sum_{i=1}^{N} w^f{}_{ji}(t)\,\varphi^s{}_i(v^f{}_i(t))\right) + \\[2mm] I^s{}_j + I^{sf}{}_j \\[2mm] j = 1,\dots, N \end{cases}$$

$$\begin{cases} \tau_{lk}{}^f \dfrac{dw^f{}_{lk}(t)}{dt} = \\[2mm] \lambda_{lk}{}^{ff} F^{ff}\left(\varphi_f{}^{fs}{}_l(v^f{}_l(t))\,\varphi_f{}^{fs}{}_k(v^f{}_k(t))\right) - \\[2mm] \gamma_{lk}{}^{fs} w^f{}_{lk}(t) + \\[2mm] \lambda_{lk}{}^{fs} F^{sf}\left(\varphi_s{}^{fs}{}_l(v^s{}_l(t))\,\varphi_s{}^{fs}{}_k(v^s{}_k(t))\right) - \\[2mm] \gamma_{lk}{}^{fs} w^s{}_{lk}(t) \end{cases}$$

$$\begin{cases} \tau_{lk}{}^s \dfrac{dw^s{}_{lk}(t)}{dt} = \\[2mm] \lambda_{lk}{}^{ss} F^{ss}\left(\varphi_s{}^{sf}{}_l(v^s{}_l(t))\,\varphi_s{}^{sf}{}_k(v^s{}_k(t))\right) - \\[2mm] \gamma_{lk}{}^{sf} w^s{}_{lk}(t) + \\[2mm] \lambda_{lk}{}^{sf} F^{fs}\left(\varphi_f{}^{sf}{}_l(v^f{}_l(t))\,\varphi_f{}^{sf}{}_k(v^f{}_k(t))\right) - \\[2mm] \gamma_{lk}{}^{sf} w^f{}_{lk}(t) \\[2mm] , k \neq l; k,l = 1,\dots, N \end{cases}$$

where $\{w_{lk}^f\},\{w_{lk}^s\}$ bonds between elements, $\{V_j^f\},\{V_j^s\}$ states of elements, $\{\lambda_{lk}^{ff}\},\{\lambda_{lk}^{ss}\},\{\gamma_{lk}^{fs}\},\{\gamma_{lk}^{sf}\}$ $\{C_j^f\}\{C_j^s\}\{\tau_{lk}^f\}\{\tau_{lk}^s\}\{R_j^f\}\{R_j^s\}$ are some parameters responsible on the learning rate and on the retrieval of system past patterns. $\{f^{ff}\},\{f^{fs}\},\{f^{sf}\},\{f^{ss}\},\{F^{ff}\},\{F^{fs}\},\{F^{sf}\},\{F^{ss}\},\{\varphi_i^f\},\{\varphi_i^s\},\{\varphi_f^{fs}\},\{\varphi_s^{fs}\}$ are nonlinear functions.

Introduced models with bond time dependence leads to possibility of new interesting phenomena. So in preliminary numerical investigations of simple models derived from (5)-(8) we found abrupt transition from one quasi-state pattern to another during operating. Remark that such transition may have evident counterparts in the many process in real large social systems. This phenomena is one of examples of punctuated equilibrium founded recently in large systems.

REFERENCES

1. Makarenko A. New Neuronet Models of Global Socio-Economical Processes // Gaming / Simulation for Policy Development and Organizational Change. J. Geurts, C. Joldersma, E. Roelofs eds, Tillburg: Tillburg University Press, P. 128–132 (1998)
2. Makarenko A. Neuronet models of global processes with intellectual elements, International business: Innovation, Psychology, Economics, 4, No. 1(6), P. 65–83 (2013)
3. *Makarenko A.* Formalization, Modeling and Anticipatory Properties in Computational Science for Sustainable Development. Electronic Preprint of EWG-ORD 2018 Workshop OR for Sustainable Development, Madrid, June 2018. 6 p.
4. Makarenko A. S. Mentality issues in the transformation processes of the postmodernity society Public Managament. № 1 (21) — January 2020. pp. 154 – 168.
5. Makarenko A. Toward the mentality accounting in social systems modeling. Proc. SAIC-2020, IEEE Publishers. 2020. 6 p.

PART 3

MODELING RESALTS FOR SOME PROBLEMS OF GEOPOLITICS

CHAPTER VIII

SYSTEM RESEARCH ON GLOBAL GEOPOLITICS AND CONFLICT RESOLUTION

Now the World becomes more and more complex in globalization processes. But fortunately globalization lead to creating new property of society-associative memory type behavior: Makarenko (1994), Levkov&Makarenko (1998). Application synergetic, informatic, system analysis allows to proposed new methodology. Our approach allows posing definition of civilization and society culture. Proposed approach allows making background for considering clash of civilizations by Hantington. Results of computer geopolitical prognoses are described. Some prognoses for post- USSR Europe are discussed. The prospects of global development prognoses and new World order with computer illustrations are considered including concept of sustainable development.

1. Introduction

The recent World became more and more complex object because of globalization process. This leads to difficulties in decision making on all decision levels from peoples to leaderships and governments. One of the questions of primary interest is future World order. There exist many subproblems in future geopolitics: one pole, many pole or distributed power, origin of new collective security organizations, the consequences of such actions as war in Persia galf, Cosovo crisis, choice of oil transportation way in Caspy region and many others. . Recently there are also a lot of questions posed by NATO enlargement.

In such situation the past experience of presidents, diplomats, experts on foreign relations is insufficient. In case of such large object as recent society one of the useful tools for understanding their properties are system analysis. Recent system analysis gives global point of view on considered object as the whole. Current system analysis incorporates achievements of cybernetics, informatics, synergetic, philosophy, biology, sociology, politology and so on. System analysis gives also practical tools for investigations, modeling and improving operating of large social systems. Till now there are many applications of system analysis as to social problems as more particular to foreign relations. But many important and principal problems were unresolved.

Fortunately globalization of recent society not only overcomplicate the society behavior. Our investigation led us to the conclusion that now society has new property - associative memory type behavior. The society can exist in small number of stable states with transition from one state to another in historical process [1-3]. The examples of such states of society are civilizations described by A.Toinby, C.Chantington or formations in Marxist's investigations. In our approach the civilizations are the stable state of global culture of society. In such case the global culture of society is understand as all-material and mental achievements of society.

Geopolitical relations are the part of society. Now all countries involved in global international community. In this community all have relations. This leads to existing associative memory property also in system of international relations.

Establishing such property allows us to develop the new methodology for considering as global as local geopolitical problems.

2. Principles of geopolitical modeling

As recognized the modeling is the part of decision support systems. There are many subjects for modeling now and in this report it is considered mainly the problems connected to geopolitics. There are some results and prospects of realization global models of entirely new type (developed since 1992 by A. Makarenko [1-3]), to the region of geopolitics. Implementations of computer programs to geopolitics were made in Dept. MMSA of IPSA of Ukraine. The models are of neuronet type and may have many consequences for traditional problems in diplomacy, politics, sociology and so on.

There are some characteristic scales in geopolitical prognosis problems. On the Fig.1 displayed the more global scale where the all countries in the World constitute complex system with many interconnections. The Europe is only the subregion of World community. Many subregions may be also in subregion Europe.

Let us describe the global principles of geopolitical modeling. For more details see [4-6]. Each countries described or by one parameter - power of state (as analogies of R. Cline) or by vector of parameters (economic, political, military, demography and so on). Remark that the power of country is the projection of real power on the block power. So if the state is large but has a little influence on another states, than the power takes zero.

The next elements of model are the connections between the states (the scalar value for scalar model or the vector of bounds in vector models). There are the two ways of evaluation of connections. On first way experts on foreign relations evaluate bounds. On second way there exists the strong mathematical formulas for bounds evaluation. The essential components of neuronet type models are learning procedure. In our case the learning images are some stable patterns in geopolitical relations in Europe. There are three more or less stable patterns conventionally marked as 1914, 1939, 1990 year situations (reconstructed from bounds and from the datum by Hand- Books on second World War, Encyclopedia Britannica, Big Soviet Encyclopedia, C.Bennet& R.Axelrod, R.Trubaychyk and so on and consideration of author). It is very important that the learning procedure implicitly take into account the notion of global culture of society as described in papers [1-3]. In particular all prehistory of foreign relations also present implicitly in model. That is past power of countries, their blocks, mentality of peoples and lieders are represented in models.

After the finding of connections and initial situations on geopolitics (say for Europe the situation after the USSR broken) the by special type formulas calculate the dynamics of interrelations and the next stable state in geopolitics. These formulas take into account the mean field influence from surrounding countries and culture as collective memory in systems. From computer calculation we can see that Ukraine have a neutral status between NATO and Russia. Remark that this configuration exist in many variants of calculations. This is because of balance of forces from surrounding on Ukraine. This balance coursed the series of steps in Ukraine policy in both (NATO and Russia) directions, which neutralized each other. It should mentioned that if the inertia parameter in model (which described the possibility of countries change the state) decreased than there is possible stable situation in Europe remembered the "MittelEurope" configuration with two blocks - around Germany and of Antante type. The model also may incorporate the changeable bounds, another initial conditions, and subdivisions on blocks and different structures of collective security systems. For example from the model it is easy understand the recent treaty between Russia and China as simple reaction of Russia on decreasing of connections of East European countries, attracting Austria to NATO and Belarussia to Russia. Calculation also displays as possible strong consolidation of enlarged NATO in one block with neutral or familiar with neutral states for former USSR countries. This is because the neutral state is hardly changeable. But if initial state of former USSR countries become more remote from neutrality than it may follows the strongest polarization in future Europe but with enlarge NATO. Also on the base of model we can calculate the vector of forces acted on unique country, new blocks of countries and so on.

3. Some further problems

Thus in subsection 2 of this chapter are described models and results on some geopolitical prognoses. Such approach allows also solving many problems in informational support for foreign (and internal) affaires on governmental level. It is well known that now NATO also is very complex organization with hierarchical structures in many levels [7]. There are many informational problems as to the structure on NATO organization as with negotiation, treatises, military power evaluation and so on. We only enumerate briefly some of the future problems for solutions by this approach.

The first package of problems consists in expert evaluations of country states, bounds between states and possible blocks collective security structure. Remark that the blocks may be defined by the clasterization procedure (see [6]). The proposed approach then permit to calculate the relatively force of different blocks and countries. Such evaluation may be useful in negotiation on military problems on disarmament, or form example on the Black Sea Fleet division. This approach is especially suitable for evaluation of military power for the countries with different army structures. Also the problem of arm forces within the country may also be solved in this approach.

The second class of problem is the problems of optimal structure of organizations (particularly for NATO). The way to considering such problems is discussed in [8,9]. Such approach is easy adjusted to the problem of different unions and to the international economical theory and practice. Moreover, the global ecological problems also may be considered in such frames (Makarenko, 1997). As the simplest application the models can evaluate the influence of future collective security system on ecological pollution in Europe.

It is supposed that all such problems should be conceded on the unified for all European countries technical bases as hardware as software. Firstly all data may by integrated in unique database system. The tools for communication may be the computer networks as INTERNET and common graphical tool say as MAPINFO. In Ukraine such unified database is created among others in the "Intellectual Systems GEO Ltd" (ISGEO). For final maps are drawing in MAPINFO system with the assistance IS GEO. The author thanks them for assistance. Author also grateful to S.Levkov, V.Melnik, A.Vlasuk for collaboration and to K.Laskavenko for the helping in creations some computer programs.

REFERENCES

1. V.Danilenko, V.Korolevich, A.Makarenko, V.Xrischenuk Selforganization in strongly nonequilibria media. Kiev, Geophisical Institute, 1992. 144 p.

2. A.Makarenko Model for the global Socio- Economical Problems. Basic Principles. Preprint. Kiev, KPI. 1993.40p.(in Russian)

3. A.Makarenko About the models of Global Socio- Economic processe. Proceed.of Ukrain Acad.of Sci.,1994. #12.p.85-87. (in Russian).

4. S.Levkov, A.Makarenko, V.Melnik, A.Vlasuk Towards the system analysis of geopolitical relations. In: Stochastic problems of optimization and safety theory. Kiev, In-t. Of Cybernetics, 1994.p. 68- 77. (in Russian).

5. S.Levkov, A.Makarenko Geopolitical relations in post USSR Europe as a subject of mathjematical modeling and control. Proceed. 7 IFAC/IFORS/IMACS Symposium: Large scales Systems. L.UK:, Vol.2, 1995. p.983-987.

6. A.Dobronogov, S.Levkov, A.Makarenko, D.Nikshich, M.Plostak. Associative memory approach to modeling geopolitical structures. //World Congress on Neural Networks, San- Diego, California, 1996. Proceed., 1996. p.749-752.

7. The North Atlantic Treaty Organization. How it works. Brussels. NATO Office of information and press, 1996. 15 p.

8. A.Makarenko Toward The Possible Origin Of Life- Cycles Phenomenon in Global Socio- Economical and Organizational System. Proceed. of Int. Conf. Life- cycle approaches to producing systems: Management, Control, Supervision. Budapest, July 1997.

9. S.Levkov, A.Makarenko 1998 Geopolitical Relations in Post USSR Europe as a subject of mathematical modeling and control; Prepr. IFAC Conference on Supplementary Ways for Improving International Stability, Sinaia, Romania, 1998. pp.89- 94.

Chapter IX

ASSOCIATIVE MEMORY APPROACH TO MODELING STOCK MARKET TRADING PATTERNS

The proposed research intends to use the ideas of stochastic Theory of Social Imitation (W. Weidlich, E. Calen and D. Shapiro, T. Vaga), and of the associative memory approach to modeling the dynamical structure of polarization relationships (S. Levkov and A. Makarenko) for modeling the stock market trading patterns. The method potentially will allow us to forecast the offer and demand dynamics of a particular security, and lead to modeling of the assets price behavior. Our approach is based on the attempt to utilize the principles of certain classes of neural networks to reveal and model the underlying structure of the real dynamical process. Also the models with internal structure of brokers are considered and results of computer experiments are discussed.

1. Introduction

Associative memory is one of the models used in Artificial Neural Networks (ANN) — field of research which has enjoyed a rapid expansion and increasing popularity among the financial analysts. This is a completely different from the conventional algorithmic model form of computation. Neural network consists of numerous elementary processors arranged in a network, each programmed to perform one identical simple processing task. Such technology allows ANN to simulate intelligence in pattern detection, association, and classification problem-solving.

Finance and economic problems solved by ANN fall into three categories [1] (1):
- Classification and prediction (analysis of bankruptcy, loan default, bond rating);
- Function approximation (valuation of assets from actual data, risk management);
- Time series forecasting (prediction of stocks, bonds, and other trading assets' prices).

It is generally recognized that Artificial Neural Systems (ANS) are most effectively applied to the problems of classification and clustering. The successful applications of neural networks include business failure prediction

[1], credit scoring and credit performance forecasting, risk assessment of mortgage application, bond rating, financial and economic forecasting. The idea here is to formulate the task of a particular forecast as a classification problem: given a set of classes (for example, bankrupt and non-bankrupt, well-performing and poorly performing firms), and a set of input data vectors, the task is to assign each input data vector to one of the classes. The input vector components are usually the different financial ratios (like net sales / total assets for bankruptcy prediction) or different parameters (like confidence, growth, anticipated gains for the stock price performance prediction). The numerous ANNs solving classification problems differ basically in the neural network configuration, learning algorithms, and number, choice, and coding of input vector components. Usually, it is hard to compare different authors' approaches to a particular problem, since they optimize the network structure and input parameters in accordance with the training and test sets of historical financial data they have chosen, and this choice is pretty much arbitrary. Nevertheless, whatever ANN approach is implemented, it is generally performing better than the conventional forecasting techniques (discriminant analysis, regression methods, statistical techniques, etc.).

Among the other potential applications which merit further research, are: portfolio selection and diversification, simulation of market behavior, index construction, identification of explanatory economic factors, and other problems requiring massive parallel processing, fast retrieval of large amounts of information, and the ability to recognize patterns based on experience. Especially interesting financial problem, where an ANN is useful, is pricing and hedging derivative securities [2]. Here, the task of the neural network is to uncover (approximate) a value function describing the relationship between inputs and outputs. It can be done due to the universal approximation property of the learning network. Moreover, certain classes of ANN can approximate arbitrary well any continuous function on a compact domain, which means that there is always a choice for the network parameters that is better than any other possible choice [2].

Another promising and already quite developed area of ANN applications is time series forecasting. Time series are a special form of data where past values in the series may influence future values, depending on the presence of underlying deterministic forces [3]. A significant portion of real-time series is generated by nonlinear processes and besides, is highly contaminated by noise. Therefore, the task of ANN is to uncover the "true" relationship between variables using its learning ability. The idea here is to break the time series into the past and future sets. Then, the network is trained and learns on the past set of data and tested on the future set to see how well its forecast fits into the real data.

While a good deal of ANN applications has focused on the prediction of stock price dynamics, it has been noted that only moderate success has been achieved to date [4].

The reason for that, to our perception, is that one of the advantages of ANN - their ability to model non-linear processes with a few (if any) *a priori* assumptions about the nature of the generating process - becomes a disadvantage here. Forecasting (if ever possible) the time series behavior with a strong stochastic component without modeling the underlying dynamical system may well result in a failure or just a random success.

As an attempt to model such an underlying dynamics, many publications have appeared recently regarding the applications of non-linear dynamics and chaos theory to the prediction of stock market behavior [5]. Most of the works in this field are either trying to apply directly the well-known facts from the dynamical chaos theory to the financial systems, or investigate the existence of dynamical chaos and its parameters in the financial time series.

As an example of applying the ANN related ideas (associative memory, in particular) to model the underlying dynamical structure of the financial markets, the work of Tonis Vaga can be cited [6]. This work is based on the theory of social imitation [7], and polarization phenomena in society [8], that go back to the famous Ising model — the model for ferromagnetism that describe the behavior of simple magnets. The Theory of Social Imitation extends it to the phenomenon of polarization of opinions in a variety of social groups. The assumption here is that individuals in a group behave similar to the molecules in a bar of iron. Under some conditions, the individuals' thinking becomes polarized, which means that they will act as a crowd and individual rational thinking will be replaced by a collective "group think" [8]. Such transitions from disorder to order and otherwise, share the same macroscopic characteristics, whether we deal with physical, biological, chemical, sociological, or financial system.

Unlike chaos theory, which seeks to forecast the stock prices time series in a deterministic (although dynamically chaotic) sense, the market hypothesis of Vaga based on the Ising model, give a method to analyze the transition from random walk behavior to periods of coherent price trends, and periods of chaotic fluctuations of market as a whole. However, the Theory of Social Imitation and Vaga's approaches give only a theoretical basis and are not intended for the forecasting of the actual trading dynamics or price movements, since it is essentially based on stationary state analysis of potential wells of distribution functions.

On the other hand, the attempts to construct a neural network-based mathematical model describing the underlying individualized dynamics of the social polarization phenomena have appeared recently in works of S. Levkov and A. Makarenko [9, 10, 11]. In those works, the analog of Ising model in the form of Hopfield associative memory network [12], was used to make the strategic forecast of geopolitical structures' (GPS) evolution and formation of blocks. The idea of the approach is to present the GPS as a network of elements characterized by the state variables describing the generalized power of a country and interconnection matrices describing the relationships between them. The reconstruction of interconnection matrices is based on historical patterns of inter-relations using a Hopfield Network Algorithm. The problem was considered of modeling the formation of bipolar and tripolar block structures depending on different initial conditions and parameters of interconnections. The key element is to construct the evolution law based upon the appropriate definition of energy of interconnections and of field of influence.

The proposed research intends to use the above mentioned ideas of stochastic Theory of Social Imitation (W. Weidlich, E. Calen and D. Shapiro, T. Vaga), and of the associative memory approach to modeling the dynamical structure of polarization relationships (S. Levkov and A. Makarenko) for modeling the stock market trading patterns. The method potentially will allow us to forecast the offer and demand dynamics of a particular security, and lead to modeling of the assets' price behavior. We would like to emphasize here, that in contrast to the existing ANN models, where the real process is considered as a "black box", and ANN is trained on the sets of input and output data to simulate the nonlinear relationship between them without actually revealing the nature and structure of the prototype process, our approach is based on the attempt to utilize the principles of the certain classes of neural networks to reveal and model the underlying structure of the real dynamical process.

2. Justification of approach

2.1. Can the market be predicted?

There is still a big controversy regarding this matter. Some of the authors think that the market is non-predictable. Their popular expression is "You can't beat the market". Indeed, evidences and academic studies of professionally managed portfolios have shown that professional investors as a group not only fail to perform better than amateurs, but that it is even difficult to find individual portfolios which have achieved performance significantly better than neutral. The others are even more pessimistic and think that institutional investors will, over the long term, underperforms the market [13]. Nevertheless, the majority of institutional investors believe that they can outperform, and therefore predict, the market; otherwise they wouldn't step into it. Besides, numerous financial analysts consider that making market forecasts does make sense (most of the endnote articles are devoted to forecasting one or other aspect of the market process).

The reason that forecasting methods make sometimes more, sometimes less correct predictions, lies, to our opinion, in the Coherent Market Hypothesis of T. Vaga [6]. According to it, the stock market has four major states: random-walk state, coherent bull market, coherent bear market, and chaotic market. The state of the market is controlled by the investor sentiment and the prevailing bias in economic fundamentals. The random-walk state, or efficient market, is characterized by low risk and, consequently, low reward. This is a period when investor sentiment is not conducive to "group think' or crowd behavior. When economic fundamentals are positive (bullish) and investor sentiment is conducive to crowd behavior, the coherent bull market emerges. This is the safest, most rewarding state of the market. The coherent bear market is also characterized by low risk and high reward and is a result of the combination of negative (bearish) economic fundamentals and crowd behavior. The last major market state identified by Vaga, is a chaotic market. During this period, a high degree of polarization exists among the investors, but the economic fundamentals are neither positive nor negative, which results in the most dangerous market state with high risk and low reward.

Not going into further details of Vaga's analysis, we can conclude that an opportunity to forecast the stock market behavior arises during the periods of coherent behavior. A similar approach can be applied also to a particular stock. The most interesting (yet more complex) problem in this case would be forecasting the transition periods from one market state to another.

2.2. Conventional theories of market forecasting

Traditionally, two approaches to asset valuation and price prediction have been used - the "firm-foundation theory" and the "castle-in-the-air theory" [14]. The firm-foundation theorists believe that each investment instrument has its "intrinsic value" that depends on the present conditions and future prospects of the firm. Consequently, an opportunity to make money arises when the market

106

price falls below or rises above this firm foundation of intrinsic value. In contrast, the castle-in-the-air theorists concentrate on people's psychology. Analyzing how the crowd of investors is likely to behave in the future and how they tend to build their hopes into castles in the air under favorable market conditions, supposedly allows estimating what investment situations are most susceptible to public castle building and buy before the crowd.

Accordingly to these two views on the stock market, there are two opposite investing techniques - fundamental and technical analysis. Fundamental analysts believe the market to be 90% logical and 10% psychological. Therefore, they care little about the particular pattern of the past price movement, but rather seek to determine the proper value of the security. It is done by analyzing growth prospects, dividends payout, level of interest rates, and the degree of risk. Once the "true" value of the company is determined, the fundamentalist can start his game, since to his beliefs, the market will eventually reflect accurately the security's real worth. There are numerous examples when this theory fails and makes wrong predictions. Apparently, this approach underestimates the role of market and its participants in the mechanism of establishing the actual asset price.

In contrast, the technical analysis suggests that all the information about earnings, dividends, and the future performance of a company is already reflected in the company's past market prices. It presumes that the price chart and the trading volume are the only information needed for correct prediction. Essentially, the main technical analyst's task is to anticipate how the other investors will behave. Therefore, the true technical analyst doesn't even care to know what business or industry a company is in, as long as he can study its stock chart. There are also plenty of cases when this theory fails. This approach obviously neglects the role of information about firm fundamentals in the price formation and focuses mostly on market effects.

Evidently, those theories are two extremes. The price generically depends on the firm fundamentals but is determined on the market through the trading process. Therefore, the adequate models of the price dynamics should inevitably consider the market participants, their relationship, and their behavior.

2.3. The role of market structure and market relationships in price formation

The financial theorists and practitioners are mostly uniform in determining who the market participants are. Basically, they divide them into the following categories [15]:

- Market makers or Specialists;
- Brokers;
- Uninformed traders (or Nice traders [16], or Noise traders [17]);
- Informed traders (or News traders [16], or Insiders [17]).

Some of the classifications, instead of informed and uninformed traders, include traders possessing special information, "liquidity-motivated" traders who have no special information but merely want to convert securities into cash or cash into securities, and traders acting on information which they believe has not yet fully discounted in the market price but which in fact has [18]. Another approach breaks them down into differentially informed traders and liquidity traders [19].

Trading takes place through the market makers and must pass through a broker. Such structure does not allow public to participate directly in the trading. Therefore, in order to understand the market mechanism, first, it is necessary to understand the relationship between market makers on one side and brokers representing their anonymous clients on the other. Moreover, as Jack Traynor (more known under the pseudonym Walter Bagehot) wrote in his famous and widely cited article "The Only Game in Town", "the market maker is a key to the stock market game". Technically, his role is to provide liquidity by stepping in and transacting whenever equal and opposite orders fail to arrive in the market at the same time. For this purpose, the market maker transacts with anyone who comes to the market. But still, any market maker has an ultimate goal of making a profit from his transactions. He always loses to informed traders; therefore the gains from the transactions with uninformed and liquidity-motivated traders must exceed these losses. Thus, the market maker can be thought as a channel through which money from uninformed and liquidity-motivated traders flow to insiders, since those who get information make the profit from the market makers, and the latter earn from the other traders who don't have it.

Another aspect that makes the market even more complicated is the broker - market maker relationship. Since the market maker's spread between bid and asked price mainly depends on the difference between his losses to informed traders and gains from the others, he will readily reduce it if the broker reveals that his client trades, for example, just for liquidity purposes. Better execution of orders means more clients for the broker. On the other hand, in order to make such relationship work, the broker also has to reveal when his client is informed, which will definitely lead to the poorer execution of his order. Thus, the broker faces the dilemma: whether to tell the specialist when his client is a news trader and perhaps, lose him, or conceal this fact and get poorer execution for all the other clients' orders. Since uninformed and liquidity-motivated traders are in absolute majority in the stock market, the broker has an incentive to reveal the informed traders. However, if informed traders were always identified, they would be forced out of the market; because the market maker would set such a spread that the advantage an informed trader has might disappear. Nevertheless, news traders *are* in the stock market, which means that they are not always correctly identified either because the broker makes mistakes, or because the broker chooses randomizing strategy when sharing the information with the market maker.

This picture of the stock market, being simplified, shows nevertheless, that the way the market participants interact with each other, their beliefs and disbeliefs, credibility and trustworthiness have considerable impact on the price formation.

2.4. Possibilities for modeling

The above analysis shows that a possibility of forecasting the market behavior may exist at least for some periods of market dynamics and for particular securities. The adequate models of the price dynamics should inevitably include the market participants, their relationship, and their behavior. The interaction of market participants, their beliefs and credibility have significant influence on the market trends. The combination of methods of stochastic theory of social imitation (W. Weidlich, E. Calen and D. Shapiro, T. Vaga), and of the associative memory approach to modeling the dynamical structure of polarization relationships (S. Levkov and A. Makarenko) represent a solid foundation for developing the model of the stock market trading patterns that would allow to forecast the offer and demand dynamics of a particular security, and lead to modeling of the assets' price behavior.

3. The modeling concept

3.1. General ideas

We present here briefly the core idea of the approach and the rough draft of the model that we are going to develop in the research. The proposed model does not pretend to be full and is intended only to demonstrate the basic ideas presented here. The development of the models follows to the frame from Part 2, Chapter VI. The formulas are the same. But the peculiarity is in interpretations of variables and parameter.

Assumptions

In order to make easier understanding of the method and to simplify the initial formulas, we consider the idealized market of one security. The trade consists of discrete steps, at which the actual transactions take place. Within each step we identify the sub steps, which describe the dynamic bidding and asking or decision-making processes for every individual. The market consists of N homogeneous participants (in future developments the homogeneous assumption obviously should be removed).

With every trader we associate the state variable $s_i \in S = \{0, \pm 1, \pm 2, \ldots \ldots, \pm M_i\}$, where s_i represents the number of shares that trader i is planning to buy (if $s_i > 0$) or to sell (if $s_i < 0$), and M_i is the maximum allowed trading volume, which represents the number of shares trader i_{is} able to buy.

With every pair of traders i and j we associate the variable $c_{ij} \in \mathbf{R}$ — the integral value of reputation that trader j has from the point of view of trader i. This value measures the degree of how well informed; trader j is in the eyes of the trader i. The large positive values of c_{ij} mean that, in the opinion of trader i, trader j is an informed (news, insider) trader, the values close to zero can mean that the trader j is an uninformed (noise, nice) or liquidity trader, while the negative values mean that the trader j is either insider who trades against the information he has in order to hide himself, or a trader who is likely to be wrong in his judgment. The reputation variables c_{ij} form a matrix

$$C = \{c_{ij}\}_{i,j=1,\ldots,N}. \tag{1}$$

that we call the matrix of reputation. The approach c_{ij} valuation will be discussed later at the end of this section.

As one of the basic characteristics of the system we introduce the concept of a vector field of influence

$$F = \{f_i\}_{i=1,\ldots,N} : f_i = \sum_j c_{ij} \frac{s_j}{M_j}, \quad c_{ii} = 0 \tag{2}$$

where f_i means the integral influence of opinions of all other participants on i trader. The intuition behind this formula is the following. The ratio $\dfrac{s_j}{M_j}$ represents the trading intentions of participant j at the current step. It shows the number of shares trader j is planning to buy or sell as a percentage of what his actual buying or selling power is. The product $c_{ij} \times \dfrac{s_j}{M_j}$ is the information about intentions of trader j filtered through the matrix of reputation. Thus, the sum (2) represents all the available to trader i information about the actions of other participants, and since it is filtered through the matrix of reputation, it is meaningful and trustworthy to him. We would like to note here, that all the other information, trader i might have, is already incorporated in his initial intentions to buy or sell s_i.

Obviously, the best strategy for rational individual will be to adjust his own initial intentions to the filtered information about others. Speaking formally, we say that every participant is associated with the information utility function, which he is trying to maximize during the decision-making process. It is done by correlating the trading decision of individual i with the corresponding value of the field of influence f_i.

Thus, we may formulate the evolution equation describing the trading dynamics in the frame of Chapter V concepts (Section 1.1 and .2. from Chapter V). We also accept the formulas (1) - (12) from the same sections.

The initial conditions for this dynamic equation are the intentions of each individual to buy or sell at the beginning of the trading step. They are formed under the influence of the sources outside the system, and represent the trader's forecast of how well the particular stock will be doing.

Given the initial conditions for s_i and known values of influence matrix, we may calculate the dynamics of the trading patterns. Such dynamics is expected to be beneficial for each trader, since it leads to the maximal utilization of the filtered, and therefore useful, information available to him.

Obviously, the system consists of protagonists with different and frequently antagonistic goals. Thus, the actions beneficial for a particular participant do not necessarily benefit the others. Moreover, each trader acts from his own interests and generally, if somebody wins, someone loses. However, all these egoistic individuals comprise the system we consider. Therefore, from the system point of view the question is, whether the defined above dynamics of every trader leads to a meaningful evolution of the whole system, or is this just a disordered, chaotic motion? The answer can be found using the analogy with the physical systems.

As the variable summarizing the evolution of the system, we introduce the concept of energy E, which characterizes the impact all the traders have had on each other in making their buying/selling decisions:

4. Research tasks and problems to be solved

Proposed approach allows developing the software and trying to understand some properties of market. Here we describe some examples of computer experiments with the models which accounting the internal structure of brokers and non-constant in time reputation of brokers.

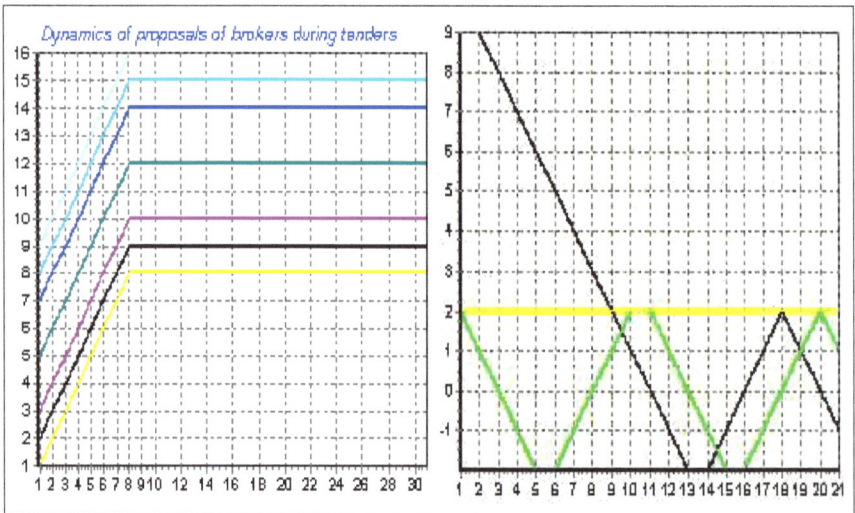

Fig 1. Modeling the market trading

The horizontal axe corresponds to the steps of trading. The vertical axe represents the intentions of different traders. The left picture correspond to stabilization of intentions of traders. The right-side picture corresponds to the case of market with changeable bonds (reputations) during trading. The right picture illustrates the possibilities of oscillations of the market. The oscillations are intrinsic for market with asymmetrically informed brokers. Moreover the market with mostly asymmetrically informed brokers may have chaotic behavior. Other very interesting phenomenon is the possibilities of sudden changes of stable trading patterns of market evolution in the case of variable reputation of traders. It may correspond to real phenomena in the market. Also it may correlate with phenomena of punctuated equilibrium in biology.

112

Of course till now our computational investigations are model with artificial date and further investigations will be interesting. But just now some prospective issues may be discussed.

First of all proposed internal representation may be considered as some correlate to ontology of market participant. Also it may be interesting for considering classical problem of reputation. At second the approach reminiscent usual multi-agent approach. The description of trader remember agent with special representation of the internal and external worlds by network structure. Also the prospective feature in the approach is the associative memory in proposed models.

Conclusion

Thus in proposed paper we consider the approach for market modeling which implement some properties of real market. The main distinctive features are the accounting of internal properties of traders. As the authors envisage, the modeling principles, described in section 3 can lead to the formulation and solution of the following problems:

8. Development of models of trading patterns for the specific markets.

9. Enhancement of the models of trading patterns with price formation models and developing the price forecast methods.

10. Numerical simulation of specific markets.

11. Establishing of the asset price dynamics through the offer/demand-price relationship.

REFERENCES

1. *Athanasios Episcopos.* Artificial Neural Networks in Financial Economics. A Brief Tutorial. — *http://www.compulink.gr/users/episcopo/tutorial.html.*

2. *James M. Hutchinson, Andrew W. Lo, and Tomaso Poggio.* A Nonparametric Approach to Pricing and Hedging Derivative Securities via Learning Networks // The Journal of Finance. — 1994. — **49**, № 3. — P. 51–859.

3. *Michael Azoff E.* Neural Network Time Series Forecasting of Financial Markets. — John Wiley & Sons. — 1994. — 212 p.

4. *Delvin D. Hawley, John D. Johnson, Dijjotam Raina.* Artificial Neural Systems: A New Tool for Financial Decision-Making // Financial Analysts Journal. — 1990. — **46,** — № 6. — P. 63–72.

5. *Chaos* & Nonlinear Dynamics in the Financial Markets: Theory, Evidence and Applications // Edited by Robert R. Trippi. Irwin Professional Publishing. — 1995. — 505 p.

6. *Tonis Vaga.* The Coherent Market Hypothesis // Financial Analysts Journal. — 1990. — November-December. — P. 36–49.

7. *Earl Callen and Don Shapero.* A Theory of Social Imitation // Physics Today. February 1974. — 27 (July: 23–28). — P. 23–28.

8. *Weidlich W.* The Statistical Description of Polarization Phenomena in Society // British Journal of Mathematical Statistics and Psychology. — 1971. — № 24. —P. 251–266.

9. *Makarenko A.S., Levkov S.P.* Geopolitical Relations in Post USSR Europe as a Subject of Mathematical Modeling and Control // Proceedings of IFAC Symposium on Large Scale Systems. London. — 1995. — **2**. — P. 983–987.

10. *Dobronogov A., Levkov S., Makarenko A., Nikshich V.* On the Neuronet Approach in the Analysis of Geopolitical Processes // Doklady of Ukranian Academy of Science. — 1997. — № 5. — P. 94–98.

11. *Dobronogov A., Levkov S., Makarenko A., Nikshich V., Plostak M.* Associative Memory Approach in Modeling Geopolitical Structures // Proceedings of Neuronet World Congress. — San-Diego, July. 1996. — P. 749–752.

12. *Haykin S.* Neural Networks: Comprehensive Fpundations. — N.Y.: MacMillan, 1994. — 697 p.

13. *Charles D. Ellis.* Winning the Loser's Game. — 2002. — 182 p.

14.*Burton G. Malkiel*. A Random Walk Down Wall Street. The Time-Tested Stategy for Successful Investing. — W. W. Norton & Company, Inc. — 2007. — 480 p.

15.*Yuk-Shee Chan and Mark Weinstein*. Reputation, Bid – Ask Spread and Market Structure // Financial Analysts Journal.— 1993. — **49**, № 4. — 57–62.

16.*Fischer Black*. Equilibrium Exchanges // Financial Analysts Journal. — 1995. — **50**, № 5. — P. 1359–1370.

17.*Albert S. Kyle*. Continuous Auctions and Insider Trading // Econometrica. — 1985. — **53**, № 6. — P. 1315 – 1335.

18.*Jack Treynor*. The Only Game in Town // Financial Analysts Journal. — 1995. — **51**, — № 1. — P. 81–83.

19.*Foster F. Douglas, Viswanathan S.* Strategic Trading When Agents Forecast the Forecasts of Others // The Journal of Finance. — September 1996. — **LI**, № 4. — P. 1437–1478.

20.*Makarenko A*. Anticipatory agents, scenarios approach in decision- making and some quantum – mechanical analogies. International Journal of Computing Anticipatory Systems. — 2004. — № 15. — P. 217 – 225.

CHAPTER X

TOWARDS the e-GOVERNMENT MODELING

1. Introduction

Recently eGovernment became more and more common technologies for society tasks and for society transformations. But practical experience in eGovernment using is far ahead of theoretical foundations of eGovernment. Before in the series of papers [1-4] we had proposed outline of the problems of eGovernment. For example we had considered the eGovernment from the point of view of system analysis [1]; some presumable methodologies for eGovernment considering [2, 3]; sustainability of society and of eGovernment [4] ; general models of large social systems [5, 6]. But for deep understanding of eGovernment and moreover for practical implementation of eGovernment systems more elaborated concepts, models and methodologies should be developed.

Thus in given paper we propose some approach for accounting mental properties of eGovernment participants, the ways of transformations and the number of related properties, including investigation of system elasticity, calculating power indexes, supply the security of the system etc.

The structure of the paper is next. At section 2 we propose the general scheme of eGovernment droving from the point of view proposed by author concepts. Some detalization of such concepts is proposed at section 3. Section 4 devotes for considering transformations in society and of eGovernment subsystem.

2. General framework

E-Government is the society part. So it should be considered in the general frames accepted for considering society and social systems. Usually in general problems of large social systems three 'pillars' had been considered:

All such components (and restrictions on corresponding recourses) also should be considered in eGovernment problems. Remark that scientific community agrees that 'ecology' and 'economy' 'pillars' have more or less developed models. But 'social' 'pillar' has less adequate models. So in discussion of general framework for eGovernment we will concentrates on the methodologies for 'social' aspects. At first stage we will accept that the models for 'ecological' and 'economical' components will supply the forecasts for 'social' components environment. (This is only the approximation because 'social' pillar has impact on other). Following approach from [5, 6] we suppose at the first approximation that he social part of eGovernment consists from N individuals with bonds between them. The individual posses own dynamics of some parameters of social type.

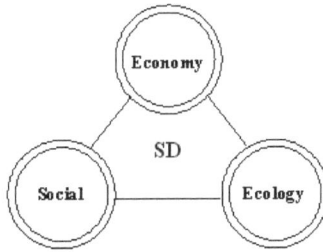

Figure 1. Three 'pillars' of social systems

We suppose that the 'Social' part of government also has the 'technical' part. 'Technical' part includes interfaces between participants of eGovernment and administrative (electronic and classical) part. For example 'technical' part may

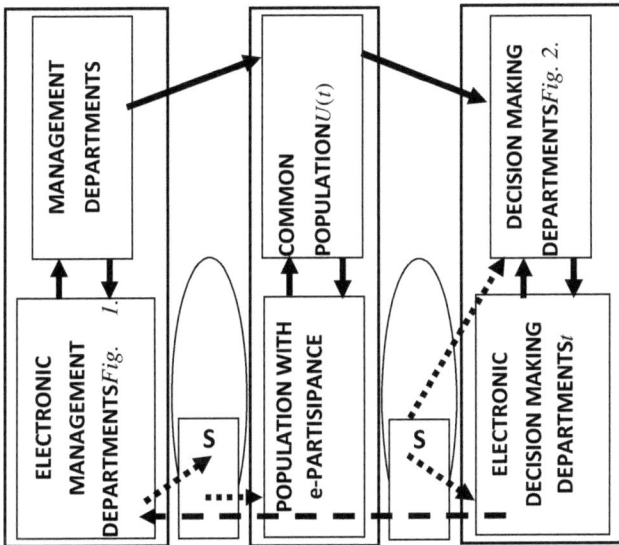

Figure 2b.. Scheme with 'classical' and 'electronic' government

include communication lines, computers, analytical and security centers personal interfaces etc. Administration may include top-level leaders, decision-making departments, data collection and processing departments, press centers and many others. Thus at first approximation the eGovernment system may be represented by schemes on the Pictures 2a, 2b. Picture 2a corresponds to traditional arrangement of government. But the Picture 2b display the origin some new aspects of government which include the 'electronic' government. The essentially new elements are individuals with access to servers (S) through

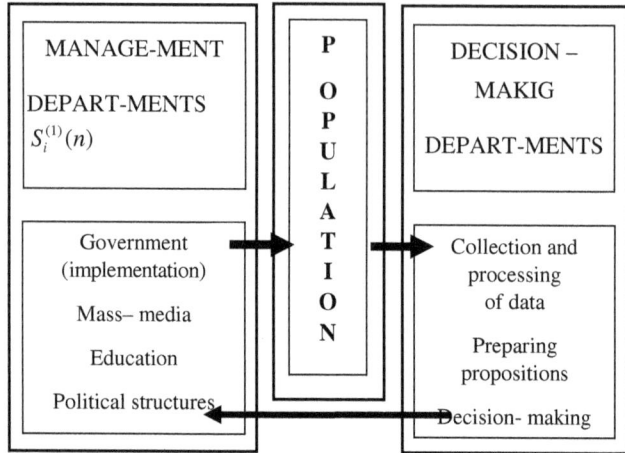

MANAGE-MENT DEPART-MENTS $S_i^{(1)}(n)$	P O P U L A T I O N	DECISION – MAKIG DEPART-MENTS
Government (implementation) Mass– media Education Political structures		Collection and processing of data Preparing propositions Decision- making

Figure 2a. Simple scheme of 'classical' government.

communications lines and separate departments for decision- making.

Of course such pictures are oversimplified. So it is possible to pose more detailed scheme which can help to understand the structure and role of eGovernment in social system. Remark that evidently hierarchical nature of considered social systems. Such pictures may also help to pose the tasks of investigation and design of eGovernment systems of different level and scales.

Of course such presumable schemes also are some approximations for real system. For example because a lack of place we doesn't show explicitly infrastructures, organizations, forms and industry, cities and villages, social networks and many others. But just such schemes allows for stress some components and aspects of eGovernment. Such pictures illustrate the different presumable scales of eGovernment systems; non-homogeneous character of systems especially of population; hierarchy in systems; interrelations and interactions between subsystems. Probably such pictures may help in classifications and ranking of eGovernment projects and necessary cost evaluation. For example the scales of projects may expand from local to the country or international level.

It had been stressed by many researchers including author [1-4] that the eGovernment development require the searching of optimal ways for design and financing of eGovernment. Recently it is impossible with applications of mathematical models and approaches. The models are necessary as for global problems (for example for sustainable development) as for searching more local regional commercial projects and solutions. Of course a lot of mathematical models exist for different components of remarked above pillars of system (it may be the goals of separate papers). So here we will concentrate on the aspects most closely related to eGovernment especially to the less formalized (just theoretically).

Namely below we will consider the components related with 'population' and 'government' blocks from Pictures. 2. Remark that usually any of components of eGovernment include as 'classical' as 'new' component ('new' means related to 'electronic' part of eGovernment). The share of 'new' components may be evaluated by some formal procedures and indexes. The fracture F (%) of population which use the interfaces (external and through PC) of eGovernment may serves as one of the simple examples. The fracture FG (%) of government departments involved in eGovernment may serves as second example. The part of power in given social system transferred to population through eGovernment is the third example. But just the task of such blocks modeling is very complex (but possible in principle for all pillars and components). For describing one presumable approach for general modeling here we will concentrate mainly on human - related tasks.

3. Short description of associative memory approach for some social problems

First of all we stress some problems related to population participants at eGovernment: 1) formation of public opinion on some issue by electronic system; 2) voting on some question through eGovernment; 3) expanding of eGovernment system; 4) evaluation of power distribution between population and administration. Below we propose for illustration the development of methodology the simplest problem. Remark that in this subsectionr we intend only to illustrate the background of methodology on the base of simplest examples.

3.1. General ideas

The general ideas coincides with general description in Chapter V, Part 2 and with formulas in them.

We present here briefly the core idea of the approach and the rough draft of the model that we are going to develop in the research. The proposed model does not pretend to be full and is intended only to demonstrate the basic ideas presented here.

3.2 One simple example in modelling with mentality and with time dependent bonds

Proposed approach allows developing the software and trying to understand some properties of society and particularly eGovernment.

One simple example of such dependence received for continuous time model for stock market. The same model useful for investigation of opinion formation and others (1):

$$
\begin{cases}
C_j \dfrac{dv_j(t)}{dt} = -\dfrac{v_j(t)}{R_j} + \sum_{i=1}^{N} w_{ji}(t)\varphi_i(v_i(t)) + I_j, \\
j = 1,\dots, N \\
\dfrac{dw_{lk}(t)}{dt} = \lambda\varphi_1(v_1(t))\varphi_k(v_k(t)) - \gamma w_{lk}(t), \\
k \neq l; k, l = 1,\dots, N
\end{cases}
\tag{1}
$$

Counterpart with discrete time also had been investigated.

Here we describe some examples of computer experiments with discrete-time models corresponds to models (10) which accounting the internal structure of participants and non-constant in time reputation of participants (Figure 3). The variables $\{v_i\}$ have interpretation as opinion of individuals and $\{w_{lk}^f\},\{w_{lk}^s\}$ have interpretation as reputation of kth agent's in opinion of lth agent.

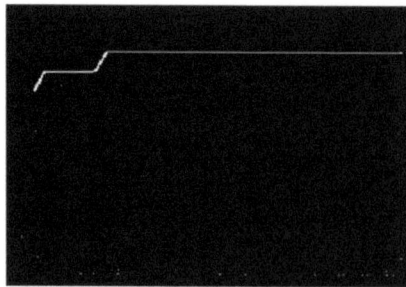

Fig. 3 Example of quasi-stable solution

First of all proposed internal representation may be considered as some correlate to ontology of participant. Also it may be interesting for considering classical problem of reputation. At second the approach reminiscent usual multi-agent approach. The description of participant remember participant with special representation of the internal and external worlds by network structure. Also the prospective feature in the approach is the associative memory in proposed models. Remark that recently we had found the possibility of multi-valued solution existing in case of individuals which can anticipate the future.

4. Some qualitative consequences of the proposed methodology of modeling large social systems

Here is one very important remark that allows us to generalize the proposed methodology and models in principle, including the problems of archetypics, sustainable development, transformation and other similar problems. The internal variables should be divided into two classes. The first class includes variables that change relatively quickly in dynamics under the influence of the environment and the inner state of the individual. Actually, the majority of current tasks of the economy deal with such variables (and external factors). But the second class includes variables that are relatively stable, such as perceptions, archetypes, development patterns, etc. These constructs can also change, but much more slowly (for example, when several generations change). Parameters of the first and second classes refer to what should be considered as components of the mentality.

As it has already been emphasized, the second class of variables allows to take into account aspects of archetypes. In particular, in the simplest case, they can be displayed for the use in the proposed models of the results of color psychological tests through the introduction of special parameters (or even one generalized parameter).

The methods are also suggested to consider the global problem of sustainable development. The idea of "economic" and "ecological" way of society's evolution can also be presented as constructs in terms of variables of the second class, i.e. as quasi-stable constructs. Therefore, the transition from the "economic" to the "ecological" path depends on the change of leading constructs of individuals. Sooner or later this will happen through education, media influence, etc.

It is also possible to assume that in the future the concept will also be useful for practical tasks of public administration. First, the concept can provide a qualitative understanding of the impact of various factors (including archival ones) on the processes in society. Also, if the proposed models are further developed and detailed, they may become part of the government's decision support systems.

Obviously, decision makers have forecasts for the future. In this case, the state of the elements in the model should depend on the images of the future, described in the internal representation. We call this case hyperincursion. Another important part of advance is the selection procedure.

Sustainable development is one of the most important problem which can be considered with propose concepts and models. As had been proposed earlier (see [3] the 'economical' and 'ecological' ways of society evolution corresponds to different attractors in the models. So the problem of SD corresponds to existence of different attractors in the models. Thus the problems of society transformation (including transition to sustainable development) follows to the problems of transition between attractors and design of new systems of attractors. Proposed models lead to many ways for such transformations. With fixed connections between elements it is possible with special external biases. But the case of flexible connections the attractors may changes, Following humanitarian sciences it may be accepted that positions of individuals in the problem of sustainable development mostly depends on the 'slow' components of internal variables and bounds between such slow changeable internal variables. Thus such objects are the task of change in transition to other ways of evolution. Such slow changeable olso have a long time processes. The patterns and other parameters can be formed in schools for childrens, universities for young students, by mass-media for populations etc. The science and knowledge is the base of such transformations of 'slow' connection of elements. The network structures of internal variables of elements correspond to existing knowledge. Thus namely the knowledge and their representations into individuals are one of the very important components of the SD problem.

The system of equations and its modifications can form the basis for the study of many problems with internal and external images of the world. We should emphasize that the right side of the equation depends on the future values of the element's state. This form is oppositely constructed with respect to the form of delayed equations. It is very promising that the structure of such a system coincides in structure with the systems studied by D. Dubois. This entails a possible similarity in properties.

Conclusion

In the proposed section we have outlined a part of the approach to modeling processes in large social systems. It has been suggested to include the properties of the mentality of individuals in society, as well as the properties of predicting individuals in the framework of a strict approach. As a result, we have obtained some new models that also take into account the properties of the individual's mentality. The possibility of including archetypical problems in mathematical models is also described. The possibilities of applying the proposed concepts to the problems of society management are also proposed. The approach is also useful for application in economic models.

REFERENCES

1. Makarenko. A.. 2006. System Analysis, Foresees and Management of E-Services Impacts on Informational Societies. *Proceed. 4th Eastern European eGov Days*, Prague, Czech Republic. 6 p.
2. Makarenko, A., 2008. Toward the building some methodic of understanding and improvement of e-Government *Proceed. 6th Eastern European eGov Days*, Prague, Czech Republic 5 p.
3. Makarenko, A., 2007. Goldengorin B., Krushinskiy D., Smelianex N. Modeling of Large-Scale crowd's traffic for e_Government and decision-making. *Proceed. 5th Eastern European eGov Days*, Prague, Czech Republic. p. 5
4. Makarenko, A., Samorodov, E., Klestova, Z., 2010. Sustainable Development and eGovernment. Sustainability of What, Why and How. *Proceed. 8th Eastern European eGov Days*, Prague, Czech Republic. p. 5 (accepted)
5. Makarenko, A., 1998. New Neuronet Models of Global Socio- Economical Processes. In *'Gaming /Simulation for* Policy Development and Organisational Change' (J.Geurts, C.Joldersma, E.Roelofs eds) , Tillburg University Press. P. 133–138,
6. Makarenko, A., 2003. Sustainable Development and Risk Evaluation: Challenges and Possible new Methodologies, In. *Risk Science and Sustainability: Science for Reduction of Risk and Sustainable Development of Society*, eds. T.Beer, A.Izmail- Zade, Kluwer AP, Dordrecht. P. 87–100.
7. Haykin, S., 1994 Neural Networks: Comprehensive Fpundations. — N.Y.: MacMillan.. 697 p.
8. Makarenko, A., 2004. Anticipatory participants, scenarios approach in decision- making and some quantum – mechanical analogies. International Journal of Computing Anticipatory Systems. Vol. 15. P. 217–225.

PART 4

KNOWLEDGE ISSUES IN SOCIETY DEVELOPMENT

CHAPTER XI

EDUCATION AS A BASIC FACTOR IN TRANSITION TO SD

1. SD idea and society

Now, based on the proposed models, we described how SD can look and how one can understand the transformation processes in these systems, paying special attention to the aspects related to the mentality. Trajectory, in which the global SD is considered, are in a space of large dimension (including all "external" and "internal" parameters). A certain mode of operation of the SNET (Social-Natural-Enviroment-Technical) system corresponds to the motion in the attraction field of a certain attractor. There are resource constraints for trajectories. These restrictions must be taken into account at all considered time intervals. The transition from an unsupported to a supported development corresponds to transitions between attractors.

Here we shortly consider the role of individuals mentality in SD. Note that in the base pictures (Fig. 7 in Chapter V) there are 3 pillars for describing the systems. It is clear that innovation and knowledge are now playing a decisive role both for the adoption of SD, and generally for the evolution of society. Usually they are included in the social pillar. However, in the future they can be (together with other characteristics of individuals carried out in a separate pillar: faith, education, ontology, work skills, etc.). Actually, many modern research on artificial intelligence, semantic networks, distributed management, organizational science, etc. are directed to this direction ([9] Watts and Strogats 1998; [6] Prigogine 2000; [8] Wallerstine 1998).

Taking into account the concepts proposed in ([2-5] Makarenko 1994, 1998, 2002, 2013), the dynamics of social, economical, political etc. systems may be described by laws with associative memory. The structure of attractors in these systems and the evolution in them is determined by the connections, patterns and previous training.

Thus, the overall process of transition from non-sustainable development to sustainable development is as follows. Non-SD mode is defined as natural resources and restrictions on their use and knowledge and internal qualities of individuals. The latter can be represented by network structures of the form of an elementary concept (representations and connections between them). With other fixed conditions, changes in these systems and components (concepts and connections) lead to a transition from non-SD to SD development path. In the simplest case (when most variables are discarded), one can imagine that, in the limiting case, non-SD and SD modes correspond to fundamentally different target settings (and their different representations in the form of network structures of ideal representations of the individual). One network structure corresponds to the "economic" way of development, and the second - to "ecological". Note that here we can talk about the anthologies of different development regimes. What then does the transition mean? Absolute transition is a complete change for everyone from an "economic" to an "ecological" style of thinking. Such a transition is, of course, an idealization, but already this "absolute transition" shows what is the result when changing the modes. Even if the change of "internal" ideal images happens instantly (that is, the mode of using resources), then the real change will still occur gradually as a transition from the initial state to the force of the model's dynamics equation.

The second version of the model, although also simplistic, is a consideration of when the change in "ideal" (desirable) representations occurs gradually (for simplicity, it can be assumed that with the same speed for all individuals, although it is not difficult to take into account the heterogeneity of these changes).

We can say that simultaneously there is a co-evolutionary process, when both the situation and the people involved in the SNET system change. Then there is a change in the landscape caused by a change in views and a change in the landscape affects the change in views. It should be remembered that the full problem of multidimensional and "ecological" and "internal" (mental) coordinates enter the common space of the problem description. Therefore, the attractors in the projection only on the ecological coordinates can look as independent of the internal variables of the object. However, the transitions between them can be determined by "mental" (internal coordinates). (Figure 4 in Chapter I just corresponds to such situations - the areas between ($G_1 - G_2$) and ($G_3 - G_4$) correspond to different attractors, and the transitions P_1 and P_2 - are determined by changes in mentality).

Already these illustrative descriptions of problems allow us to consider (and, first of all, put them) on the basis of formal concepts and equations. It should be stressed that transition to global SD depends strongly on the acceptance of SD idea by society. So the first of the tasks of transformation is to change an "ideal" representations of the World in the individuals. It is important to study what proportion of the population should adopt new concepts for the transition to SD, what is the dynamics of the transition, what is the distribution according to individuals, how it depends on the new "ideal" structure, its difference from the old ideal structure. It is also possible to take into account the process of the generation change due to the loss of "old" individuals and the emergence of "young" people in the system for whom the process of obtaining new "ideal" representations comes from a "pure" structure (without replacing the "old" concepts - in "young" concepts at first simply no). Note that the above process is also suitable for modeling other problems about the behavior of social systems (previously the author had already discussed civilizations and formations, the birth of cities and states, the economy, the production of the future, the Government and much more).

Of course, the results given in this paper are, first of all, general and rather abstract in comparison with the needs of forecasting and managing real social systems. However, even such first steps made it possible to obtain interesting applied results (geopolitics, stock markets, etc.).

Thus in proposed subsection some new investigations of sustainable development aspects had been proposed. The system analysis of SD problem stressed the role of restrictions on resources for general SD problem. The illustrative pictures in the Part 1 allowed to better understand the need of accounting of restrictions. Proposed formal definition of sustainable development problem may hope to fill the gap between the qualitative descriptions of SD processes and application of strict methods of operation research. Application of proposed formal definition allows to reduce the problem of sustainable development to the problems of modeling and optimization of systems with constraints, which is the prerogative of operation research. Special class of models with associative memory for social systems had been described. Such class of models allows to consider also the internal (mental) properties of individuals which may be important for understanding of general sustainability property. Absolutely new is also attracting anticipatory properties for formalization of sustainable development (especially of strong anticipation).

2. SD models and SD transitions taking into account internal variables of individuals

In this subsection we give elementary descriptions of the most complex problems in the study of problems related to the fact that SD is most dependent on the consideration of the properties of people and society as a collection of individuals. The most important tasks are the understanding of sustainable and non-sustainable ways of society's existence and then understanding of the transition between them and management, planning, foresight of such processes. Again, the integral model of society would be necessary in all its completeness, and all existing models can be used to construct such a model (or a complex of models). But as it was repeatedly stated above, the most convenient models are the network structure and the associative memory property (from the classes given in ([2-5] Makarenko 1994, 1998, 2002 , 2013) and further from the development).

As has been repeatedly suggested in this paper, we begin with the simplest case, taking into account the internal structure of individuals. For an understanding of the concept, let us begin with the simplest geometric illustrations that allow us to lead to rigorous formal statements and possible interpretations. We give here the structure of the model (and even society) and in parallel the structure of the SD problem with its optimization nature. So, we accept that society consists of a large number of individuals with connections between them. In this case, as indicated, there are various pillars. Each of the pillars corresponds to laws that describe their behavior, and each of the pillars can correspond to a network description. Therefore, at a certain stage, we will simplistically represent these states at a given instant of time as the states of the blocks in Fig. 7 above in Chapter 4, Part 1. Dynamics of blocks can be represented as a sequence of states of the elements of blocks at different instants of time (in the simplest case at discrete moments, but this is not a fundamental limitation). The laws of the dynamics of variables can be given in any known form. However, the most appropriate laws are laws in the form of associative memory and its implementation by neural networks. Now in the implementation of the construction of the proposed models, each individual has a certain idea about this environment (as far as his knowledge of the state of affairs, breadth of horizons, education, etc.). In addition, the individual has an idea of what state of the environment he represents best at certain intervals. It is important that models of another type can also be represented in the form of models with associative memory. Each of the individuals has all these parameters. Therefore, society in the elementary approximation can be very schematically represented as it is shown in Fig. 1 above.

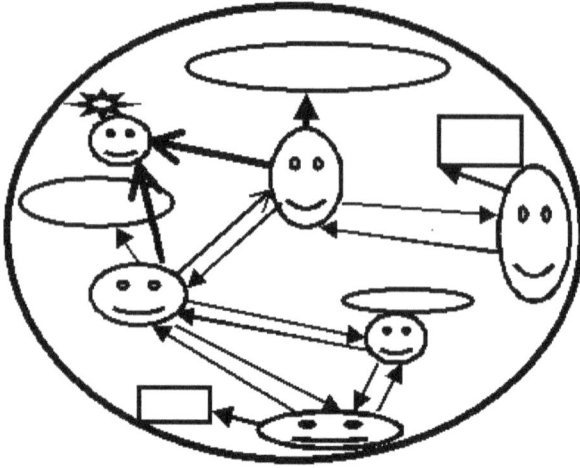

Fig: 1. Society as a collection of individuals. Ellipses, rectangles, a star represent the internal representation of the external world The individual with the star - the representation of the child and the one-way arrows towards him - the nurturing influence, for example from the parents.

Society is a collection of such individuals and connections between them. Note that within the framework of the circuit in Fig. 1 it is possible (and should) include the individual's views about his own place in society (selfreferencing, reflection and also what is important for sustainable development of society, the idea of a supported development). Ideally, then, its modeling is the study of the change in the parameters of all components (environment, pillars, individuals) over time with the help of dynamic laws adopted in models. It is clear that in the fullness of the dimension of the parameter space and the number of equations for their evolution can be enormous. Therefore, as is customary in the study of complex systems, simplified models for various subprocesses are considered to obtain an understanding of the functioning of the entire complex system. Variants of simplified schemes can be different. First we point out one model that can allow us to investigate it by analogy with models in theoretical physics. Let us consider a society located on a regular lattice structure (in the simplest case, on a straight line), where individuals are located at lattice sites. Such statements are now often considered in the tasks of socio- and econo- physics. In the variant, when only one pillar is considered, the state of the elements (with the values 0 or 1, or the vector of possible values, or even the whole space for the values) together are external variables and an "external" description, and for them in In this case it is difficult to call the equations of evolution "external". If the model is more developed and takes into account both the internal representation of individuals about the "external" variables of the system and the wishes for their best configurations, then one can imagine that these representations are written in "internal" equations. This formulation of the problem resembles the problems of quantum field theory, where there are observable dimensional variables in both the usual space of time and hidden dimensional variables that are concentrated in additional micro-spaces of very small size (of the order of the Planck length). These ideas, perhaps, began to work with Kaluza-Klein models. In our case, we can consider the analogy of the "internal" variables of individuals with "hidden" parameters in physics and set the dynamics problem: write analogues of Hamiltonians or other defining functionals, investigate evolution.

3. Education as a basic factor in transition to SD

Now, based on the proposed models, we describe how SD can look in such systems and how one can understand the transformation processes in these systems, paying special attention to the aspects related to the mentality. Considering the proposed model concepts, we recall once again the system described in P. Trajectory, in which the global SD is considered, are in a space of large dimension (including all "external" and "internal" parameters). A certain mode of operation of the SNEN system corresponds to the motion in the attraction field of a certain attractor. There are resource constraints for trajectories. These restrictions must be taken into account at all considered time intervals. The transition from an unsupported development to a supported development corresponds to transitions between attractors. Let's see what role the questions of mentality play in this. Note that in the base pictures (Fig. 7 in Part 1) there are 3 pillars for describing the systems. It is clear that innovation and knowledge are now playing a decisive role both for the adoption of SD, and generally for the evolution of society. Usually they are included in the social pillar. However, in the future they can be (together with other characteristics of individuals carried out in a separate pillar: faith, education, ontology, work skills, etc.). Actually, many modern research on artificial intelligence, semantic networks, distributed management, organizational science, etc. are directed to this direction ([9] Watts and Strogats 1998; [6] Prigogine 2000; [8] Wallerstine 1998). Taking into account the concepts proposed in ([2-5] Makarenko 1994], 1998 , 2002, 2013), the dynamics of such systems is described by laws with associative memory. The structure of attractors in these systems and the evolution in them is determined by the connections, patterns and previous training. Recall that all this can be interpreted as a movement along some potential landscape, which is formed depending on the links between the elements. In the formation of this landscape, all the elements of the description are involved in the overall model (including all pillars): ecology, industry, economics, social structure, knowledge, the individual's views on the state of the external world and himself in it and the ideal (desirable) state of the world and the individual. In models with a single component (for example, geopolitics], market trades, public opinion formation), when models resemble generalizations of the Hopfield model, the correlations between links teaching in the previous way and the potential landscape have been well studied (Haykin 1994 [1]; Sutton et al. 1988 [7]). It is known that there the laws of dynamics can be derived from the functional - the analogue of "energy." It also clearly establishes the role of connections in the formation of a potential landscape and its changes in the course of changing links. In more complex cases, especially taking into account the internal structure of individuals in principle, one can also start from a functional that defines a potential landscape, deriving dynamic equations from the conditions for minimizing such a functional. However, this is a very difficult task for complete models of social systems (in fact, then a system of axioms for such functionals must be established). Therefore, the complexity of the models will be due to phenomenological models, but taken in the class of models with associative memory, so in principle one can postulate the presence of a potential landscape (or even explicitly construct in some of the simplest cases). Thus, the overall process of transition from non-sustainable development to sustainable development is as follows. Non-SD mode is defined as natural resources and restrictions on their use and knowledge and internal qualities of individuals. The latter can be represented by network structures of the form of an elementary concept (representations and connections between them). With other fixed conditions, changes in these systems and components (concepts and connections) lead to a transition from non-SD to SD development path. In the simplest case (when most variables are discarded), one can imagine that, in the limiting case, non-SD and SD modes correspond to fundamentally different target settings (and their different representations in the form of network structures of ideal representations of the individual). One network structure corresponds to the "economic" way of development, and the second - to "ecological". Note that here we can talk about the anthologies of different development regimes. What then does the transition mean? Absolute transition is a complete change of the idea of ??an ideal device for everyone from an "economic" to an "ecological" style of thinking. Such a transition is, of course, an idealization, but already this "absolute transition" shows what is the result when changing the modes. Even if the change of "internal" ideal images happens instantly (that is, the mode of using resources), then the real change will still occur gradually as a transition from the initial state to the force of the model's dynamics equation. The second version of the model, although also simplistic, is a consideration of when the change in "ideal" (desirable) representations occurs gradually (for simplicity, it can be assumed that with the same speed for all individuals, although it is not difficult to take into account the heterogeneity of these changes). Then we can say that simultaneously there is a co-evolutionary process, when both the situation and the people involved in the SAET system change. Then there is a change in the landscape caused by a change in views and a change in the landscape affects the change in views. It should be remembered that the full problem of multidimensional and "ecological" and "internal" (mental) coordinates enter the common space of the problem description. Therefore, the attractors in the projection only on the ecological coordinates can look as independent of the internal variables of the object. However, the transitions between them can be determined by "mental" (internal coordinates). (Fig. 4 in Chapter 2 just corresponds to such situations – the areas between (G1 – G2) and (G3 – G4) correspond to different attractors, and the transitions P1 and P2 – are determined by changes in mentality). Already these illustrative descriptions of problems allow us to consider (and, first of all, put them) on the basis of formal concepts and equations. So the first of the tasks - how much does the change in "ideal" representations. It is important to study what proportion of the population should adopt new concepts for the transition to SD, what is the dynamics of the transition, what is the distribution according to individuals, how it depends on the new "ideal" structure, its difference from the old ideal structure. It is also possible to take into account the process of the generation change due to the loss of "old" individuals and the emergence of "young" people in the system for whom the process of obtaining new "ideal" representations comes from a "pure" structure (without replacing the "old" concepts - in "young" concepts at first simply no). Note that the above process is also suitable for modeling other problems about the behavior of social systems (previously the author had already discussed civilizations and formations, the birth of cities and states, the economy, the production of the future, the Government and much more). Of course, the results given in this paper are, first of all, general and rather abstract in comparison with the needs of forecasting and managing real social systems. However, even such first steps made it possible to obtain interesting applied results (geopolitics, stock markets, etc.).

Conclusion

Of course many scientists have proposed some OR investigations of sustainable development including some mathematical approaches (the examples may be proposed and analyzed in full paper). But as we hope our investigations may open the way to further formalization of SD concept. In fact, these considerations allow us to reduce the problem of sustainable development to the problems of modeling and optimization of systems with constraints, which is the prerogative of operation research. But is essentially a new accounting of system descriptions multidimensionality, especially because of mental properties accounting of social actors. Absolutely new is also attracting anticipatory properties for formalization of sustainable development (especially of strong anticipation). Also we describe some experience in application for real problems

REFERENCES

1. Haykin S. Neural Networks: Comprehensive Foundations, MacMillan: N.Y. (1994)
2. Makarenko A. Anticipating in the modeling of large social systems – neuronets with internal structure and multivaluedness, Int. J. of Computing Anticipatory Systems, 13, P. 77–92 (2002)
3. Makarenko A. Neuronet models of global processes with intellectual elements, International business: Innovation, Psychology, Economics, 4, No. 1(6), P. 65–83 (2013)
4. Makarenko A. About models of global socio-economic processes, Reports of the Ukrainian Academy of Sciences, No. 12, P. 85–87 (1994) [in Russian]
5. Makarenko A. New Neuronet Models of Global Socio-Economical Processes // Gaming / Simulation for Policy Development and Organizational Change. J. Geurts, C. Joldersma, E. Roelofs eds, Tillburg: Tillburg University Press, P. 128–132 (1998)
6. Prigogine I. The Networked Society, J. World-Syst. Res, 6, No. 3, P. 892–898 (2000)
7. Sutton J.P., Beis J.S., Trainor L.E.H. Hierarchical model of memory and memory loss, Jour. of Phys. A: Math. Gen., 21, P. 4443–4454 (1988)
8. Wallerstein I. The Heritage of Sociology, The Promise of Social Science, Presidential Address, XIV-th World Congress of Sociology, Montreal, July 26, 1998, Part 2, http://fbc.binghampton.edu/iwprad2.htm (1998)
9. Watts D.J., Strogatz S. Collective dynamics of "small-world" networks, Nature, 393, P. 440–442 (1998).
10. Banathy, B.H. (1998). Designing Social Systems, *Proc. 14 th Europ. Meeting on Cybern. and System Research* (ed.R.Trapple), Vienna, April, 1998. Vol.1, p.241- 245.
11. Beckenbach F. (2001). Multi-agent modelling of resource systems and markets: theoretical considerations and simulation results. In *"Integrative systems approaches to natural and social dynamics"* (P.M.Allen ed). Springer- Verlag , 2001. Pp.401-419.
12. Beradze, M., Makarenko, A., Mnatsakaniani, M., Chikriy, A. (1999). Optimal control problems in regional geopolitics. *Vestnik Charkov Politechnical University*, 1999. n.72. pp. 8-12. (in Russian).
13. De Tombe, D&Rosendal, B. (1998). Cooperative and interactive Policy Making: Some History views. *Gaming/Simulation for policy Development and Organisational Change* (J.Geurts, C.Joldersma, E.Roelofs eds. Tilburg

Univ. Press. Pp.71-79.

14. Dobrowolski J., Wagner A. (2002) Long- term Polish Experience in Co-operation of Scolars, NGOs and Local Communities – Perspectives of the Participation of Knowledge-based Society in Sustainable Development on Global Scale. The Books of Abstracts, WACRA-EUROPE 2002 conference, Brno, Czech republic, August 2002. 6 pp.

15. Ecimovic T., (2002) "System Thinking and Climate Change System" , SEM Institute for Climate Change. Isola, Slovenia

16. ESWGTT (2002) Euroscience working group of technology transfer. Ukrainian branch. www.kiev.technology-transfer.net

17. Euroscience (2002) Joint Conference of EARMA and Euroscience, Budapest, Hungary, 14-16 June 2002. www.euroscience.org

18. Hopfield J.J. (1982) Neural networks and physical systems with emergent collective computational abilities. Proc. Nat.Acad.USA, 1982, vol.79. n. 5. Pp.2554-2559.

19. Global Change Newsletter, October , n.55, International Geosphere – Biosphere Programme, 2003.

20. ISCVT (2002) Institute of Sustainable communities. http://www.iscvt.org

21. ISAGA (1998) *Proceed. Int. Society Gaming and Simulation Annual Conf.* (J.Geurts, C.Joldersma, E.Roelofs eds.) July, 1997. Tilburg University Press, Holland. 1998.

22. Klestova Z., Makarenko A., Samorodov E. (1999) Towards interdisciplinary methodology for regional change management. Place for human and place of human in problems. Materials prepared for WACRA 2000 conference (Viplitino, Italy, September 2000). 16 pp.

23. Klestova Z., Makarenko A. (2002) Conflict of interest between Eastern and Western scientific systems. *OPRAGEN* (UK), 2002. Vol. 8, n.4.

24. Levkov, S &Makarenko, A. (1995) Geopolitical relations in post USSR Europe as a subject of mathematical modelling and control. *Proceed. 7 IFAC/IFORS/IMACS Symposium: Large scale Systems.* L.UK: Vol.2. p.983-987.

25. Makarenko A. (1998a). New Neuronet Models of Global Socio- Economical Processes. In *"Gaming /Simulation for Policy Development and Organisat. Change"* (J.Geurts, C.Joldersma, E.Roelofs eds.), Tillburg Univ. Press, 1998. pp.133-138.

26. Makarenko, A. (1998b). Global economic models of associative memory types for considering sustainable development. *Proc. 13 Int. Conf. WACRA-*

Europe, Madrid, Spain, 18- 23 Aug, 1998. Righner-Hepp edition, Muenchen, 1998. 10 pp.

27. Makarenko, A. (1999). Anticipatory properrties of participating of production systems and approach to their modelling. *Proc. ASI'99 Conf: Life cycle Approaches to Production Systems. Management, Control a*nd *Supervision*, Leuven, Belgium, September, 1999.

28. Makarenko A. (2001) Education and technology transfer in informational fields as the part of globalization. In *"Lecture Notes in Informatics. Vol. P-2".* (H.Mayr, M.Godlevsky eds.), GI- Edition, Bonn, Germany, 2001.

29. Makarenko, A. (2002). Anticipating in modeling of large social systems - neuronets with interrnal structure and multivaluedness. *Int.J.Comput.Anticipation Systems*, 2002. Vol.11. 16 p.

30. Makarenko A. (2003) Sustainable development and risk evaluation challenges and possible new methodologies. In:Risk Science and Sustainability: Science for Reduction of Risk and Sustainable Development of Society, edited by T. Beer and A. Ismail-Zadeh. Kluwer AP, Dordrecht, 2003. ppp.87-100.

31. Makarenko A., Klestova Z. (1999). A new class of global models of associative memory type as a tool for considering global environmental change. In *"Environm. Change, Adaptation and Security"* (S.C.Lonergan, ed.),1999.Pp.223-228

32. MIT (2002) MIT System Dynamics Group. Sloan School of Management. Cambridge, USA. http://sysdyn.mit.edu/sd-group/home.html

33. Spangenberg J.H., Omann I., Bockermann A., Meyer B. (2001). Modeling Sustainability -European and German Approaches. In *"Integrative systems approaches to natural and social dynamics"* (P.M.Allen ed). Springer-Verlag , 2001. Pp.481-503.

CHAPTER XII

GLOBAL EDUCATION AS MAIN SUSTAINABLED RESOURCE AND MAIN MOTIVE FORCE OF SUSTAINABLE DEVELOPMENT

Usually the education as institute of society had been considered as the tool for supporting sustainable development idea spreading. In most cases the sustainable development was considered in context of ecological, natural, mining, biodiversity saves. But now in the age of globalization, post-industrial society and informational technologies the intellectual abilities and knowledge become the main resource of survival and sustainable development. So in this report it is proposed to stress in the searching of sustainable development main stream intellectual abilities and education as the main resource for the future. And namely this resource (education) needs special attention in sustainable development problem solution and strategic planning.

As general background as practical consequences will be discussed in this report. It is planned to consider some possible scenarios and general modeling concepts. Relations with science, society and innovations will be described. Some practical recipes on such issues will be proposed. First is connected to creating European Research Area and European Education Area. Second important practical consequence is the needs of saving high level of education (just fundamental) in former USSR countries (including Ukraine) and saving different types of education institutions (education diversity). Some regional (Eastern European) local problems also will be discussed. Discussed problems may constitute the background for formulating propositions for topics of research for WACRA community.

1. Sustainable Development Concept - recent state

Before the discussion of the interrelation between sustainable development and education it need to make some review on SD concept. The concept of sustainable development has a long history of its essential components. First of all it needs to remark many natural science investigations and ecology. Another part is demography (may be since the works of Maltus). First explicit implementation and first working tool for considering SD is system dynamics since the work of Forester, Meadows and others ([11] Iscvt, 2002; [23] MIT, 2002). Important role also has played the concepts and the models of the World by I. Wallerstain, B. Fuller, A.Frank. One of the past focal point of SD was world leaders conference at Rio- de Janeiro (1992), and last Summit at Johannesbouyrg (2002), where some definitions and prospects had been formulated.

But the experience since 1992 had followed to necessity of further improvement in concepts (see many conferences: ([8] Euroscience, 2002) and others). There are many reasons for this. Of course main is permanent changes in recent world closely connected to global processes. But it exists some intrinsic problems in SD which force to further development of approach. First of all the main definition of sustainable development is verbal and conventional. A little number of quantitative approach exist (system dynamics and some types models for modeling large- scales processes - ([24] Spangenberg et al., 2001) and multi-agent approach ([2] Beckenbach, (2001);[11] Iscvt, (2002)). The leak of full operational models follows the shortage of sustainable development indexes ([24] Spangenberg et al., 2001; [11] Iscvt, (2002)) which needs for practical planning. Remark that all above also follows to confusion between stable and sustainable development.

Thus from one side it exist a large amount of literature, investigations, databases which should be incorporate in educational courses and developing of methodology of SD teaching. From another side the more general and developed concept of SD is need with the goal to consider the teaching of SD as one of the features of transformation processes in the society.

So present report is devoted to considering of some such issues. A useful auxiliary tool for such consideration is some model concept proposed by author and explained in next section.

2. New approach to considering sustainable development

Here we very briefly describe some new concepts for considering SD ([16, 17] Makarenko, (1998); [13] Klestova&Makarenko, 1999; [21] Makarenko,2003). Sustainable Development (SD) is very complex concept, which has deals with all aspects of real life. Recently many scientists (and also the author) shear the belief that only interdisciplinary approach with different points of view and methodology can solves the problems of SD. But the available solutions presumably will be received in future and now under development is the processes of consolidations of different approaches. The methodology of author is based on cybernetics, synergetic and mathematical modelling. There exist much literature on SD. Roughly speaking it may suppose that there exists discrepancy between the natural resources and between determined by economics and history way of their exploitation.

How can we describe and understand this two ways of development (economical and ecological)? As we suppose the way of development may be described as unique very complex object which incorporate economical, ecological, cultural, political and another aspects. For example we should take into account climate change ([6] Ecimovic, 2002), general bio-sphere as complex nonlinear object ([10] Global Chamge Newsletter, 2003), social aspect in SD implementation ([5] Dobrowolski&Wagner, 2002). It follows from such components considerations the next aspect (may be one of the important)- mentality. Assuming the postulate that the development ways is usually some very stable structures we can pose the problems of changing this ways.

The analysis of large-scale systems from different point of view: cybernetics, informatics, economics, synergetic, mathematical modelling forward to the conclusion that in our case the deductive method of investigation - from global to particular problems. First of all it describes briefly the global models of society proposed by author since 1992. Such models have the associative memory properties as in neurones.

The whole model may be very complex and expensive because it must contain a lot processes in details. But even global principles shed some light on dynamic of transition processes and thus can help in business. For example, the society can go from one global structure to another by two ways: evolutionary or by revolution. Revolution can be described by fast rupture of bonds and is unpredictable and bad for business. Evolutionary way is long and demands patience. Yet on such global level there are phenomena of life- cycle type. For example, the change of social formation may be considered as the change of "patterns" in such models. In such cases some features of structures stay invariant and some features changes. Remarks that the nonsimmetric bonds cause the chaotic oscillations overlapped on cyclic processes. The Lotka-Volterra description of competition of types may be the consequences of global model.

3. Possible applications to educational process

Here we posed short schemes how the educational process may looking following the papers ([16, 17] Makarenko, 1998, 2001; 2003; Klestova et al, 1999) and the approach of models with internal structure of elements ([20] Makarenko, 2002).

One of the important components of the global society is education – global and local. The understanding of such problems recognized since 80 years of past century (see for example the reports of Roma Club). The educational problems will become one of the key factors in sustainable development problem.

First of all let us consider the notion of educational situation. Recent world became more and more complicated object. It is recognized that now society as whole is in the transformation stage and the transformations accelerate. In such situation all possible tools for good operating are need. One of such tool is developing approach of education and particularly gaming and simulation. But for implementation of such goal there need deeper understanding of education in the society future development.

Before building the methodology improvement and moreover models it should consider else the possible place and role of anticipatory properties. For such goal it should to sketch very schematically the structure the society as entity and presumable place of education, gaming and simulation tools in general picture of society. The society consists from elements, agents and interconnections between them. The interconnections mean the informational flows, knowledge, belief, needs of educational staff's team and their perception on educational space, learning agents and education learning. One of the main bonds is the interinfluence of designer's team and potential participants in education event. This picture (or rather 'pattern' of educational process) is very approximate but we suppose that it can help in further discussion. Education problems are large-scale problems and thus have the properties of large- scale systems - namely associative memory property.

Namely designer's team knows precisely the desirable result of education and more particularly precise goal of gaming. They should prognozing the behavior of individuals in virtual roles under the influence of disturbances from education environment and controlling efforts from supervisors of education. We call this as first level of anticipation. In this simplest case we assume that gaming environment reaction is known for organizer before the gaming event.

In our concept creating education event looks like the constructing the desirable environment and role- models of participant. We should remark that only in a little number of events the strict or formalised patterns are known before the event ([4] De Tombe&Rosendal, 1998). But we suppose that such patterns established in the flow of event. The example is international negotiation. Then such established pattern influences on participants of gaming and changes some their mental structures. So some results of education may be following: 1) Extending the horizon of predicting as in space as in time, 2) Learning the new possibilities inside existing horizon, 3) Short- living changes in mentality patterns in brain, 4) Long- term changes of mentality constructs. This poses the interesting problems of bond relaxation times, optimal implementation of education strategy, influences of different learning tools and so on. Remark that some such changes correlate very well with existing concept of 'Cone of Abstraction' by R.Duke ([12] ISAGA, 1998). For example considering of participants horizons of prediction looks like the 'Cones of Abstraction' beginning on individuals and directed upwards. We should stressed that such patterns in education space may represent the non-existing or prohibited in real world situations. Moreover in such case we can suppose the unexpected training situations as in explosively developed cyberspace concept. So it may present also potentially dangerous for society situations. The classical example is electronical games with virtual marder and their impact on mentality.

4. Some practical experience of teaching to sustainable development

New speciality 'social informatics' will help in understanding and spreading SD ideas. Social informatics considers the problems of receiving, transformation, investigation, and modeling and explores the informational flows in large social systems and their models. Social informatics is complex interdisciplinary approach and consolidates the deep knowledge from mathematics and physics, computer sciences, management and humanity sciences. It should be stressed that the concept of sustainable development was posed as one of the milestone in this specialty. We hope that our students should 'to thought globally in solving local problems'.

Technically we realize in many stages. At first semester we introduce the general concept and some bright examples of sustainable and unsustainable behavior. The deeper understanding on SD the students received on the more developed and formal courses especially in the discipline 'Mathematical modeling of social process'. We should remark that namely exploiting the models support the deepest understanding. But unfortunately it is a little full-developed model, especially accessible in Ukraine. In such case one of the solution is free Internet accessible models ([11] Iscvt, (2002); [23] MIT, (2002)). Besides, for SD teaching we may use existing models of particular phenomena: social, economical, ecological, natural. We may remark especially the system dynamics ([24] Spangenberg, 2001; [23] MIT, (2002)) and multi-agent approach ([2] Beckenbach, (2001)). The only problem is to design the useful scenario for their application. Remark also that our models are well adjusted to teaching SD. Moreover some problems on global problems processes may be reformulate as standard optimal control problems on the base of our approach ([3] Beradze et al., 1999). Another components of educational process consist in involving the students in investigations through the research works from the 3-2 courses of learning.

And finally about some global education problems. Till now we have told mainly on the teaching of students. The yet more global problem is future society structure. Now the term 'Social Design' is revisited ([1] Banathy, 1998). Proposed models may help in such global consideration and understanding. So we may anticipate the possibility of global gaming and simulations for leader's community or for the countries populations with the goal of searching New World order and reaching. And next it is necessary to develop special educational projects which should involved the adult population in SD realising by INTERNET as interactive tool and through mass media especially through TV.

5. General problems of SD and education connections

Here we discussed some another aspects related to SD. The sustainable development may have different space and time scales. Very approximately we may remark next space scales: Local region (city); Geographical region of the country; Country; Transboundary region; Continent; World and time scales: <5 years; 5-10 years; 20-50; centuries; millenniums. Of course the objects of sustainable development may be not only whole large- scale system but also separate elements of infrastructure.

It should be stressed that the problems of small and medium scales already had solved by some methods because of evident practical importance. Remark that sometimes GIS (geoinformational systems) were one of the technical tools for analyzing, visualization and decision support. But already at this levels there are a lot of questions: how to change the way of development (or how to sustain the 'good' way), how to overcome the bifurcation points (gradually or with collapses), what may be the emergent structures after the transition and will be the emergent structures better then past. A lot of problems of such kind (unfortunately with 'unsustainable development') support the past 10 years of Ukraine experience. Some examples:

Example 1. Nonreformed industry in Ukraine and saving old technologies.

Example 2. Tendencies to destroy the former educational system in Ukraine

Example 3. Fall into decay of scientific and technology transfer

Example 4. The strengthening of executive power by suppressing the initiative and free enterprise (in all fields of interest).

This and many another problems follow to necessity of considering SD processes in hierarchical systems with particularly antagonistic goals for different levels, subsystems, elements and so on. Our approach also allows considering such problems. The real problems may be transformed in mathematical problems on attractors and their structural stability. And vice versa the mathematical solutions may be interpreted in terms of real socio- ecologo-economical phenomena.

But the problems of global sustainable development and global education had a very little considerations, especially qualitative. And presumably it was just an absence of formulating of problems. It was only some works only on restricted problems of technology development.

So here we posed some frame for global education problem consideration. According recent discussions there are two ways of development - economical and ecological (see some review in ([16, 17] Makarenko, 1998, [22] Makarenko&Klestova, (1999)). Two possible attractors correspond for these two ways in our approach. The main question: What is the role of education system and knowledge creation in development of such ways? From one side the educational system is the consequence of society structure, history, economics. But from another side the education and knowledge is <u>main</u> resource for development in postindustrial society. One aspect (clearly formulated by P.Druker) is especially important. Briefly, he told that in postindustrial world the main resource would be knowledge and information (more important then minerals, raw materials, fuels and so on). And one of the main components of such recourse is the carrier of knowledge that is individual. So the education of individuals is the process of improvement of resourse.

Let us consider some consequences from such point of view. 1) Then the most developed industrial countries will demand more and more such resource. 2) The stores of this resource may be received from less developed countries. 3) The concentration of resourse may be different in strong dependence of working education system.

And only the development of knowledge allows supporting the development under the pressure of growing consumption and energetical expenditure. This is implemented by supporting possibilities for searching new resources (at first energetical and mineral and also organisational). Without the development of fundamental knowledge it is impossible also technical development. (Remark that in parallel it also lead to new dangers ([14] Klestova&Makarenko, 2002)). We should stress that the new knowledge are created in many geographical regions, cities and by different individuals and primary research teams. So we should say about multicreativity systems and wrong solutions in educational

144

field may break the chain: knowledge - technologies - support and increasing of life level. Such broken in chain may lead to depopulation familiar to one in some scenarios by Forester and Meadows. All this forces to posed the problems (sometimes quantitative) in SD including the general problem on risks from educational fields to global development. After formulating of strict background such problems may be considered by methodology of decision- trees (familiar to risks in large systems, for example in power plants and have investigated in Project UNTC GR(J)33).

5.1 Large power – plant development and risks

Another problem of practical importance is connected with operating such large object as nuclear power plants. Recently there exist many investigations on the risk of operating of such large object. But it is known that there are a lot of difficulties in such risk counting. First challenge is the large number of different type technical and natural elements with different types of behavior. Second problem consists in the presence of many human elements in the whole system - as current personal as staff of plant as large social object. Usually existing methodologies take into account technical elements of the system and only from a small number of types.

Our methodology can help consider some such problems. First of all this concerned the problem of imitation of operators functioning and their decision-making. Second the approach may help in considering different scenarios of functioning in critical and normal situations. This may be understood in the frame of the ideas described in subsection two of this paper. Third important problem is the description of power plant operation as the whole complex object. And also important problem is evaluating the probabilities of initial defaults of elements and its influence on next flow of the processes. Usually such probabilities had been received from numerical statistical data. But unfortunately frequently such initial events are unique without previous statistics and special methods need for evaluating probabilities of its origin. In such case the approach from methodology of large complex systems presumably may help in such investigations. Remark the development of investigation mentioned in this subsection may constitute the background for considering another large natural systems with many different element and scales and with the involvement of human elements.

6. Large scale social systems and some their problems (country level)

Now we will discuss as the illustration of the ideas above. Here we consider mainly the country level and especially the problems of developing countries with stressing the Ukrainian experience as background. For all that we will try to stress some most important domestic aspects but in global context. Remark that such list of problems is the result of previous discussions and the system analysis. Also some efforts have been applied to resolve the problems in the experience of NGO Atlantic Council of Ukraine. It is not the secret that now developing countries has a lot of serious problems. Them partially connected or to the historical non -development or to the transformation from one state of country to another (as in former USSR countries). There are a lot of investigations on such issues and many concepts, models and recipes have been proposed.

At the first level of considerations the problems are evident: economical, political, the human rights, ecological, health care, poverty and many others. But deeper analysis follows to the conclusion that common peculiarity of developing countries is the shortage of democracy and civil society. The consequences are the lack of adequate to recent challenge infrastructures, lack of power structures balances, lack of public opinion accounting in the management of country. Also some negative properties of population present: paternalism, non- - activity, some old restrictive stereotype, and non - sustainable development, lack of enterprise and lack of environment for enterprise development. The most important consequences of such way of development are some obsolete way of population thinking (and mentality models of the world). Moreover the old internal structure of such societies partially reproduces such obsolete thinking in young generations. Namely such mental structure and internal structure of developing society are the sources of failure of economical and political reforms in our countries. Remark also that non - optimal top- level management in such countries implicitly has also background in the population consciousness. Of course the diversity of cultures in general since (by A.Toinby) leads also to diversity of domestic conditions and historical ways of development.

Thus to improve society in developing countries in is necessary 1) to reconstruct the infrastructures in society, 2) to reconstruct the mentality of population and leaders.

Many tools exist for such goals: direct forcing for task 1, education of new generations for task 2, economical stimulation for both tasks, natural (isolated) evolution of country and many others in dependence on the scale of the problem considered. Also the target groups of transformation process may be different from bottom to upper level. Remark that unfortunately frequently the international efforts on developing countries are directed on top levels of governance without deep reconstruction of bottom levels, infrastructure and mentality. Analysis of existing tools for transformations follows to the conclusion that in the country problems above one of the most suitable tools in namely gaming and simulation because namely GS deals with reconstruction and mentality patters changes. But classical education also may serve as useful mechganism undere special conditions.

This follows to absolutely new theoretical and practical problems in education (incliding GS) on SD and more generally in globalistics because the scales of such education should be huge and never considered quantitetilevly before (on the author opinion). For understanding we describe next example. It is known may be since A.Rappoport that for the acceptance of innovations in some field of activity it is necessary to have about 20% adepts of innovations. On the analogy in country problems education on SD should reconstruct about 20% of population. That is for example in Ukraine the auditorium of education should be at leas about 10 millions peoples, or special self- organizing hierarchical GS should be designed. Remark that now the most large world actions has the same or just fewer scales (for example see antiglobalists actions). The new problem is also investigation of SD education influence on the country and the limits of reconstruction power of large scale reconstructing gaming and simulation (LSRGS) and more generally reconstructive education.. Of course the power LSRGS depends strongly on the domestic economical, political, cultural conditions and also should be the subject of theoretical investigations. Also it is known that usually education can change the mentality structure of participants in their memory (in brains). In the case of LSRGS we may say about collective memory of society, so the new problems on short, minor, long term changes in society memory should be considered.

We should stressed that such problems are new and needs new investigations by SD and political experts community, but mathematical modeling is one of the (or may be unique) tool for considering such complex object, doing virtual experiments and designing the education and GS events. The multi- agent approach and author's models are good technical tools for such investigations. Of course it needs also special investigations on necessary resources and financial base, considering the different possible scenarios which according (Makarenko, 2002) are intrinsic for large social systems, risks evaluations and collaboration of international and domestic specialists on SD and education.

Conclusion

Thus in proposed report we have considered (but not all) some problems on interrelations of sustainable development and education. It allows making some conclusions and recommendations.

1. The problems of sustainable development should be represented in educational courses at high education. The list of issues may be next:

- Globalisation process and its concepts and models
- General description of sustainable development concept.
- Space and time scales in SD phenomena
- Examples of sustainable and unsustainable development
- Applications of modelling to SD phenomena
- The sources for SD considerations: databases, references, models, INTERNET sites
- The technical tools for decision support including GIS.
- Of course the volume of lectures may be different - from some short lectures within another courses to special discipline in curricula of management, decision making, sociology, economics, computer science, physics, biology.

2. It needs to extend essentially the collection of tools and methodological approach to teaching SD problem. It may constitute the background for some European projects. For example:

- Creation of computer educational laboratory on sustainable development.
- Creation of computer courses on SD of different levels and for different target groups.

3. Development of investigations on global SD concept and global education.

4. Development the educational projects on involvement the adult populations in the SD problems.

It may be implemented in the frames of the projects:

- Development the methodology of changing and formulating the public opinion on SD problems in EC countries.
- Development the methodology to attract public opinion to problems SD (this is especially important for East European countries).
- Development the pilot projects on visualization SD problems at TV.
- Development the programs for intensive exchange on SD education between regions, countries, universities.
- Searching the roles of SD education in creating European Research Area.

REFERENCES

1. Klestova Z., Makarenko A. New class of global models of associative memory types as tool for considering global environmental change. Preprints of NATO Advanced Research Workshop 'Environmental Change, Adaptation and Security', Budapest, Hungary, Oct.9-12, 1997. 15 pp.
2. Makarenko A., Samorodov E. The problems of informational- analytical support of Caspian Sea- Black Sea region. Proceeds, Conf. Black Sea- Caspian Sea Region: Conditions and Prospects for Development, Kiev, June 26-28, 1998. P218- 226 (in Russian).
3. Klestova Z., Makarenko A. Modeling and control of the infection process in industrial cattlebreeding. Prepr. IFAC Workshop 'Mathematical and Control Applications in Agriculture and Horticulture', Hanover, Germany, Sept. 28- Oct.2, 1997. P.213- 217.
4. Haykin, S. 1994. Neural Networks: Comprehensive Foundations. MacMillan.

CHAPTER XIII

ENVIRONMENTAL CHALLENGES, BIOTECHNOLOGY PROBLEMS AND THEIR INFORMATIONAL- ANALITICAL ASPECTS

The new tools for biotechnology as whole is presented. It is consider as processes of real situation description as new models for dynamic investigation. Proposed models are neuronet type and allow considering technology transfer process. Also some aspects of informational data base for biotechnology transfer is considered.

1. Introduction

Now the common place in scientific investigations and peoples conscious in developed countries is recognition of globalization and complexification of society life in the World. There exist many challenges for mankind in XXI century: environmental pollution, resources exhausting, energy, water and food shortage and many others. The concept of sustainable development was originated to overcome such difficulties. Earlier we propose some approach for considering sustainable development as pattern of global object (society plus environment). Our approach allows considering problems in large socio-ecologo- economical systems [1-3]. The biotechnology and particularly plant biotechnology are part of sustainable development problems. So we discussed some aspects of biotechnology implementation in large social system and particularly in Ukraine. Remark that biotechnology is high technology and we should consider distribution of biotechnology as technology and innovations.

We will describe some ideas, which may be useful for some aspects of biotechnology transfer from developed countries to poor, from research laboratories to consumer, and acceptation new technologies by community.

In the first section of paper we consider very schematically one new concept in investigation such complex object as society and biotechnology in them. The background of model is the system of elements of society or biotechnology and bonds between them. Such description already was proved is useful for another applications. The examples are epidemiology, sustainable development and geopolitical prognoses. As we suppose such approach may be useful in application biotechnology.

2. Some Phenomenological Considerations

In this section of paper we will described some framework for considering and modelling biotechnology industries as a whole and as the part of society. This subject is adaptation and description of approach from the papers [1-3].

First of all we try to describe the problem subject on empirical level. Initially we will consider situation in unique region, country, and district and so on with many elements of biotechnology industry, large population and environment. The environmental elements are: sun, earth, lands, water resources, forests, fields, roads. The populations elements are towns, villages. The industrial elements are biotechnological agricultural complexes, factories in towns. As elements we can consider scientific institutions, mass media organisations, educational and administrative organisations.

There are a lot of interrelations, connections, and influences in recent society. Roads connect the towns. Industrial factories influence the environment. Mass media, scientific institutions have influence on population, industrial infrastructure and vice versa – population produces influences on mass media for example. Environmental elements change the population.

A little number of elements above are displayed on the Fig. 1.

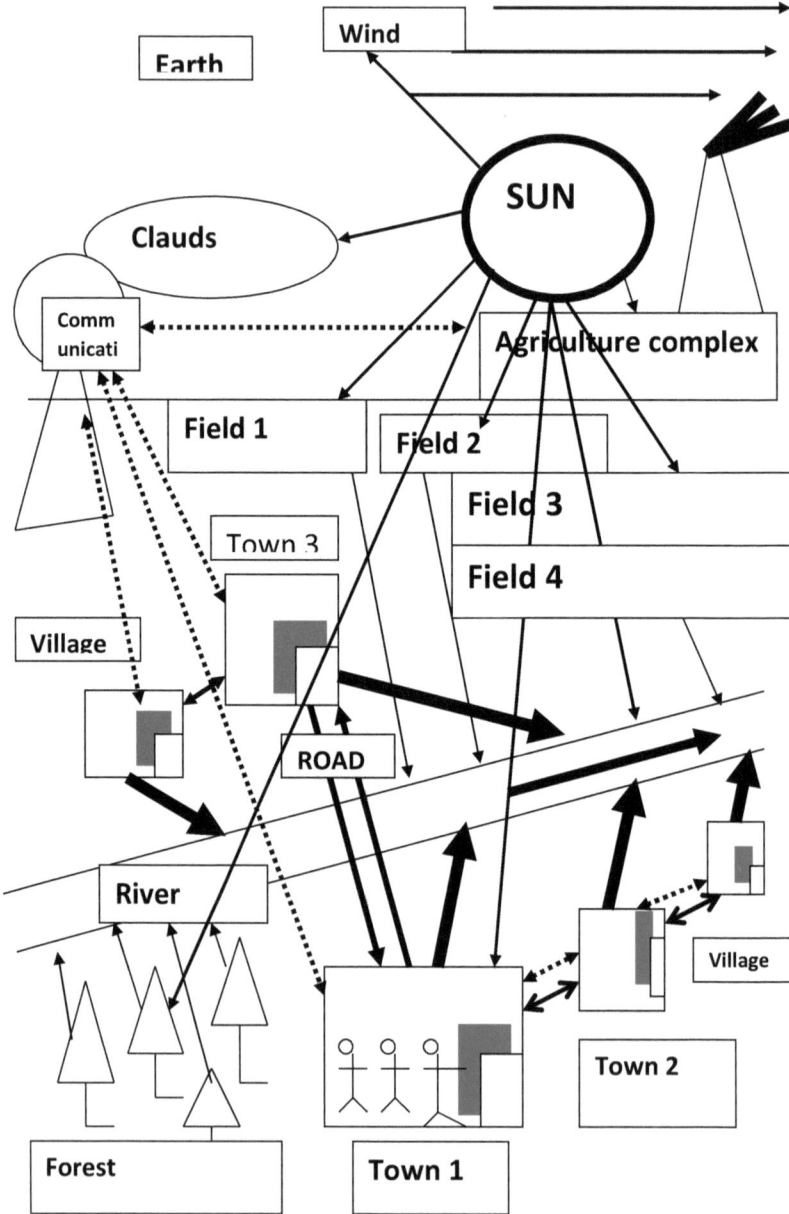

Picture 1.Some elements and bonds in real world

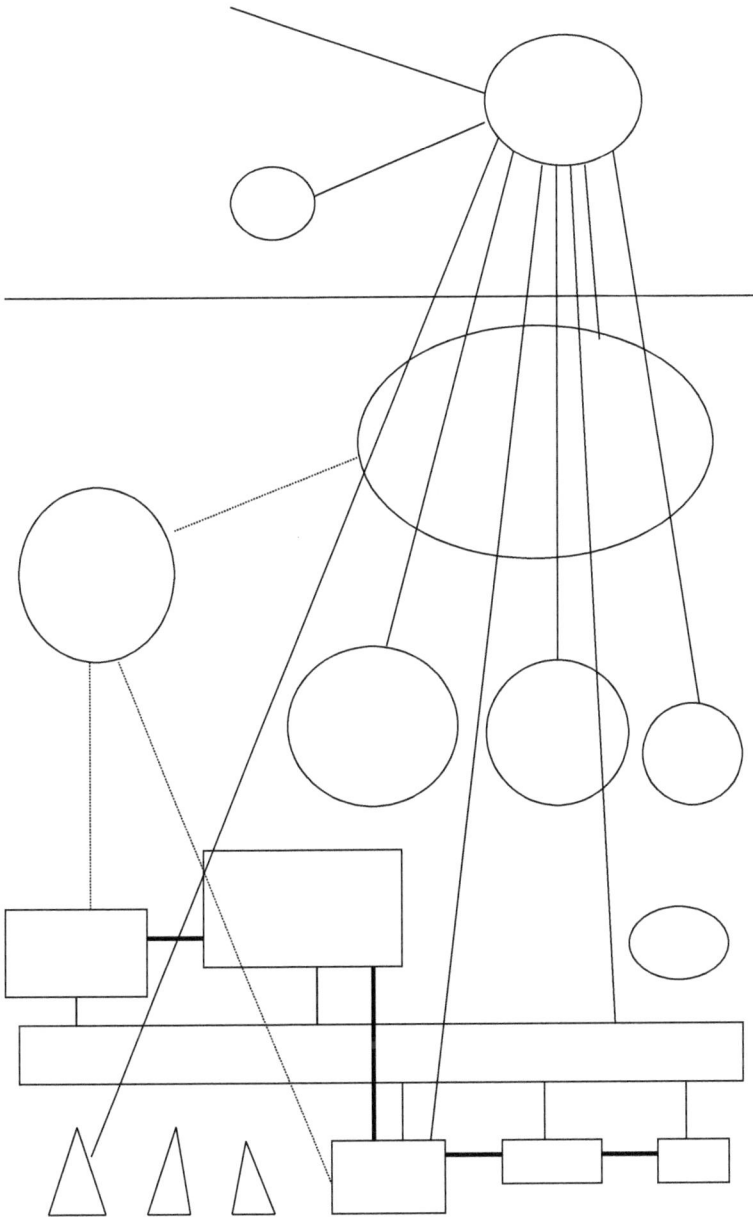

Picture 2. Networks of elements and bonds

The black boxes within towns are the industrial factories. The black arrows on the Figure are the influences of towns and villages on the river. The dashed lines are the communicational interrelations between population, mass media, organizations and so on. The second step in developing our approach consists in transition to abstract description of region, country, and district. In abstracting processes we should introduce basic elements and their description. Fig. 2 presents the skeleton of such abstraction.

Different rectangles, ellipses, triangles correspond to different elements of reality from Fig. 1. Lines of different type on the Fig. 2 correspond to different connections between elements. Remark that Fig. 1 and Fig. 2 are only the scheme of real situation. For example we dosn't display existence of many parallel networks. In reality existing of many regions leads to many examples of Figures like Fig. 1 or Fig. 2 with bonds between them.

3. The principles of new models construction

Now we proceed to more mathematical description. First of all we must select the elements of model and laws of evolution for state of elements in model having in mind simultaneously the necessity to take into consideration natural, ecological, and some exogenous factors.

So first basic component in our methodology is element of large socio- ecologo- economical systems: individual, organisations and institutions, firms, countries and so on described by parameter set s_i, i=1,2,...,N, N- number of elements. But there exist next basic elements in developed society. Namely there are many interrelations between the elements of large systems (and not only in social but also in natural systems).

So in sufficiently developed society elements have many complex connections. We assume that there are connections between i and j elements. Let J_{ij}^{pq} is the connection between p components of element i and q component of element j . Then we call all set of connections between N elements as bond matrix. For example, the bond between components of material state may be the flux of goods in some production chain. Bonds between inner components of subject for example can describe the influence of one element on another and so on. Also the bounds on different levels may have the different types.

4. Dynamics in proposed models

Thus the set $Q = (\{ s_i \}, \{ J_{ij}^{pq} \}, i,j = 1,...,N)$ characterises actual state of society as a whole construction including both elements and bonds between them.

Analysis of recent models for media from sets of elements and bonds shows the resemblance of such society models to neural network models. Remark that neural networks are widely investigated in cybernetic, biophysics images processing, physics and so on. Let us remind concisely the property of systems with associative memory in the theory of image recognition [4]. Such systems include many elements and recognise small number of images by evolution of element states to the remembered patterns. These patterns are attractors of system. Images remembering are ensured by bond modification in learning processes. May be most simple and usable is the Hopfield model.

Coming back to the socio-economical- ecological models we may assume that patterns in associative memory models correspond to the global structure (civilisation, states, life- cycles of goods, industrial technology). Connections between elements alter in the development process. As the first step in model selection it is possible to use the Hopfield model analogous. Then the dynamics of model is defined by proper strict rules. In simplest models such Hopfield's there exist some global minimum for some function E and system tends to go to their minima. Every minimum in E corresponds to stable 'pattern' in $\{s_i\}$ distributions.

Of course for biotechnology especially interesting are relating to biotechnology elements and bonds in description above. As examples we can remark specific biotechnology industrial chains, biotechnological scientific networks, governmental agriculture departments and so on.

5. Informational aspects of biotechnology implementation

It is evident that the approach above should be founded on extended database on elements and bonds description. Remark that biotechnology is high technology and we should consider distribution of biotechnology as technology and scientific innovations. The biotechnology development in large social systems and particularly in Ukraine should accounting related information: social, political, economical, demographical, ecological. So there exists need in considering some informational aspects of biotechnology transfer.

First aspect is informational. It should be stressed that recently because of great volume of information the information should be preprocessing and saved in suitable for consumer forms. The biotechnological information has evidently geographical dimensions. For example anybody needs the list of consumers and producers of plant production and tools for production frequently with real physical coordinates. All this follows that the best tools for such database are recent Geoinformation Systems (GIS). There are a lot of GIS and Data Base in western countries. In Ukraine the number of GIS applications was much smaller. Nevertheless now the situation is changed. There are some GIS and computer programs in Ukraine for such purposes with special attention for post-Chernobyl situation. The authors of paper and our colleagues from Institute of Applied System Analysis and from Intellectual System Geo Ltd. have access to many informational sources distributed in many open publications. As example we can mention the Atlas of C137 pollution in Europe, economical, demographical and many others. Especially interesting for biotechnology transfer are data on veterinary preparats, vaccines, and agriculture productions. It should be stressed that forms of GIS data are especially suitable for our approach. For example the description of elements in Fig. 1 and Fig. 2 for real situation are usually saved in different electronically database in governmental, educational and commercial organizations.

Second item concerned the problems of biotechnology introduction in industry and agriculture. As follows from Ukraine experience one of the main question in technology transfer in Ukraine is accounting the domestic peculiarities (especially mentality). Our models of global socio- economical systems allow consideration the mentality influence on acceptance new biotechnological products by leaders, populations and industry and agriculture managers. In some electronically publications we discussed the possibilities of creation the networks and infrastructure with the help of European organizations such as Euroscience, European Working Group of Technology Transfer, EPBN, WACRA Europe and so on. Thus it should be considered possible connections of such networks to existing European electronically networks.

Conclusion

Thus in proposed chapter we very briefly described the possibilities of new approach in considering such complex problem as biotechnology transfer. We consider some steps of building models in abstraction processes. Next we described the intrinsic property of large system- associative memory. This follows new models origin of neuronet type. Such considerations lead to needs in Geoinformational Systems Applications. So we described also some pure informational aspects of biotechnology transfer.

We hope that further development of biotechnological databases in connection with our models will give practical tool for biotechnology transfer.

REFERENCES

1 .Makarenko A. New Class of Global Models of Associative Memory Type as Tool for Considering Global Environmental Change. Paper prepeared to WACRA-EUROPE 15 th conference (Madrid, 1997).

2 .Makarenko A., Samorodov E. Problems of Informational-Analitical Support of Black/Caspy regional development. Proceed Int.Conf. "Black Sea/ Caspy Sea Region: conditions and prospects for development. Kiev, June 1998. Pp.218-228.

CHAPTER XIV

UKRAINIAN BIFURCATION POINT IN INFORMATIONAL TECHNOLOGIES AND HIGH EDUCATION

The present state and possibilities of future scenarios is considered for Ukrainian education system. For better understanding some general problems are discussed. Globalisation, sustainable development, interaction of cultures and international relations are under the consideration. Some consequences and prospects for Ukraine are shown. Possibilities of modelling, prognozinges and decision - making are proposed.

1. Introduction

Recently it is evident that Ukraine as the state is in conflict situation as in international aspects (between Europe and Asia) as in internal conflicts in the situation of scenario of development searching. Remark that the solution of these domestic problems will influence on the level of international stability in united Europe. Information technologies, automation and control are parts of society. But now IT is presumable main source of innovations and transformations in recent (and future) society. So in present paper we will discuss such problems on the basis of recent methodologies, models, and concepts. Also the materials and issues of different meetings, conferences, exhibitions, publications had been exploited (SWIIS, EUROSCIENCE, IMACS, IFAC, ATA, EARMA, ISAGA, iNEER, CeBIT 02, 03, 05, WACRA Europe, EPAC, Ukrainian).

2. General patterns of informational technologies and high education in the globalization

For the discussion on local practical problems and their solutions as usually it is necessary to have in mind a general tendencies, challenges and properties of global systems. So here we in brief remark some current tendencies and possible background for solutions (many details are in current publications).

Globalisation. Now all recognise that the world became more and more complicated with many interactions between states, regions, institutions and individuals (mainly because of informational technologies). Globalisation destroys the national borders and leads to creating more or less homogeneous spaces: informational, economical, educational, and so on. This follows to needs in planning and prognosing on cooperation forms in sphere of IT and HE. Globalisation presumably follows to the improving international stability. But globalisation also poses new problems of world order, the legitimacy of international organisation and on national's suverenity. In the author's models ([7, 8, 10, 11] Makarenko, 1998, 2001, 2002) future global state is emergent attractor in some network models.

Sustainable development. Since Rio - de Janeiro (1992) it recognised the necessity of new way for humankind development - with preserving resources for future generations and with 'ecological' thinking. On the contrary now the society develops at 'economical' way with profit as main goal. In the models (Makarenko, 1998, Klestova, Makarenko, 1999) SD is another possible attractor in the society state. 'Ecological' way should to reduce the power of international conflicts and instability because many of conflicts are the result of the struggle on resources. But the tendencies are that IT and HE will be the main renewal resource in SD. This follows to necessity to apply the main principle if SD to IT and HE. It is interesting that from such point of view at some future stages we may anticipate the conflicts around such resources (especially around education and clever young peoples considered as the resources for industrial countries). This paradoxically may have also negative consequences for stability through stagnation of developing countries.

Future intelligence manufactory. Another one important aspect globalisation is future industry organisation. It needs special investigations with qualitative counting the scenarios of development (see ([7] Makarenko, 1999). But presumably the future manufacturing will be flexible, with virtual production chains, transnational and with leading role of knowledge and information transfer. The science should prepare the frames for such new organisation. But the HE should be prepared to disseminate such innovations. Remark that knew organisation may in principle improve international stability by reduction of permanent conflicts between national industries.

Interaction of different cultures. One consequences of globalisation are deep penetration of different cultures. Earlier the border between cultures (and civilisations) had been indicated mainly geographically. Now we see mixture of the cultures also created by mass- media, immigrations, economical and other networks. The science, education, society organisation are some of the culture dimensions. In analogies with biology we may suppose that for the stability of the system the 'diversity of cultures' is important. This follows to the problem of preserving 'domestic' cultures. From another side the regions with intensive

160

interrelations of the cultures are 'creative' zones, where innovations originate. One example in policy - Turkey. Thus one of the goals in planning the development of IT and HE should be search the optimal portion unification/national features. High education also should be ready and adapted to the exchanges of cultures of education and industry. The considerations above were general and further concretisation need in application to real problems. In next sections we will discuss problems of European and Ukrainian level.

3. Science, informational technologies, technology transfer

Now we briefly pose the description of concept of science and technology followed from the works ([6, 8] Makarenko, 1998, 2000, [2] Klestova, Makarenko, 2002) and some consequences. The science is described as the complex subsystem of society.

Conflicts of West/East interest in science and scientific infrastructures. The scientific infrastructure as the part of culture has own peculiarities in different countries. Historical difference between Eastern and Western science and education organisation exist. Long time just after USSR broken such infrastructures worked practically independently. Now the process of interaction increase essentially.

At first the education system of every European country (including former USSR states) is stable infrastructures, slowly changeable and historically originated. Every country has own peculiarities. In particular, in former USSR states we still have high level of fundamental education with abstract background. This may be essentially different from the case of western countries where the education now is more connected with industry. In Eastern European countries the high education systems still produce a large number of clever and well-educated young specialists. The domestic industry in our countries is frequently in stagnation and requires a very little number of new specialists. In principle this surplus may help to fill up the needs of western countries, especially in high tech fields (the example is USA). But for such goals preliminary adaptation of young specialists, searching potential working place and involvement of domestic universities are necessary.

Modelling of information diffusion and science development. Such model concept for science allows consideration of many new interesting problems (see (Makarenko, 2001). Now we remark some another. For practical goals it is necessary to know what is the real tendency in innovation spreading and especially characteristic times of the processes. Technological innovation spreading usually was considered by the diffusive models. But the social innovations (including changes in education and science) had been hard objects for modelling. Proposed network models are well adjusted to such problems.

The difficult problem is to find the useful form and volume of young graduates exchange process. This may also constitute the topic of discussion and may be counting from models. We suppose the existing of the optimal number of involved in international workplace graduates. For example Ukraine has a lot of graduates every year and they may presumably to destroy educational system of middle European countries. From another side for recovering such resource some part of graduates should go to the domestic educational infrastructure. Also some scientific and technological environment in domestic countries needs for sustainable development of high education. So this is the subject for optimal control problems. The modelling of educational process requires mentality accounting and considerations internal structures. The simplest way consists in representing image of World in the individual's brain or in model as collection of elements and bonds between elements ([6] Makarenko, 1998). In such World pattern there exist place for representing individual himself with personal beliefs, skills, knowledge, preferences.

Former USSR countries. Current state of IT and HE. There are a lot of publications on such issues in Russian and Ukrainian journals on science policy. Also the pattern is reconstruction from personal experience, multiple conversations with colleagues, and compare with experience of western colleagues, participation at conferences, workshops and exhibitions (including CEBIT 2002, 2003, 2005). All this lead the author of report to conclusion that now the infrastructure of education and science in former USSR countries are at bifurcation point when the future way of development is chosen. Numerically HE constitutes large part of social life. There are a great number of young people who wish to receive high education. There exist a large number of universities and institutes with good past international reputation and good (and sometimes world) level of education. The same may be recognised for science and science in the fields of IT. But really the high- technologies industry in former USSR countries reduced essentially. There are a lot of reasons for such phenomena, but may be the main is the quality of governance and the power of old infrastructures in these countries. As the consequence of such reductions of high- tech demands nor young specialists nor investigations doesn't receive domestic applications. As the consequences the IT and HE doesn't receive enough financing. So the young people, researchers should search foreign orders (in better case or to do nonqualified job). Because of little salary in education and science the young doesn't intend to work as education and scientific staff. These follows to the growing old the staff and in visible

162

prospects to destroy all education systems. Sometimes as the solution the education units (departments, faculties, and universities) reduce the educational level (the bright example - preparing a huge of 'managers' in former technical universities). This is one of the choices in bifurcation points.

Remark that on the author's opinion the main solution in such circumstances is close international cooperation and involvement at 'grass' level in globalisation processes. Such involvement's should also lead to reducing international instabilities and may serve as 'pilot' involvement before presumable economical and military integration. Fortunately now the new possibilities are created.

4. Some current trends in IT and HE

European Research Area. Now in Europe new infrastructure is created - European Research Area ([1] EUROSCIENCE, 2003-2020). It is planned to make the zone without borders for research projects and partially supported by EC through the payments of member states. As the result the science will became more subnational and pan European.

Bologna Protocol. Since Sorbonne Declaration (1998) it was signed Bologna Protocol which poses the goal create to 2010 year a European Educational Space with unification of certificates, easy mobility, unification of education principles and many others.

Black Sear - the Region for cooperation. Now new prospective region for scientific and education cooperation is implicitly and spontaneously formulated. Namely Black Sea Region, which formally includes Bulgaria Georgia, Romania, Russia, Turkey, and Ukraine, is prospective for cooperation (including other interested countries from West and East Europe). The great interesting experience of interrelations of cultures and education systems has Turkey (as example sees Dohu and Isik University).

EUROSCIENCE Open Forums 2004 - 2020. The non-governmental international organization EUROSCIENCE (EUROSCIENCE, 2003-2020) plans to make forum for discussion on science and educational problems at Stockholm - Munich – Barcelona – Torino – Dublin - Triest 2004 - 2020.

5. Large IT and HE systems as factor of society transformation and as socio-technical object

Here we pose some remark on the large-scale infrastructures, which may serve as the tools for society transformation and reducing the international tensions. And in post- industrial society their significance should increase.

Education system and international relations. Educational system is one of the main (ore the main) tool for society transformation. For such tasks the system should be ahead the usual practice of society as in concepts as in implementation of ideas. Different scientific organisations especially in technical fields should help in such concept development. It is interesting that the model of educational unit development strongly depends on the scenarios of international relations and on international stability. Some different patterns for development of such unit exist useful for different scenarios (the author supposes to prepare separate publication on such issue with model considerations).

Geoinformational Systems (GIS) of governmental level. From the beginning of their origin computer geoinformational systems (GIS) had been useful tool for representing a large volumes of information. Further this direction in building and application GIS has been developed. But with the enlargement of GIS scales in applications (see the growth of power in MapInfo, ArcInfo and others), it had been evident that GIS is not only the technical tool but became the phenomenon of social importance. It was recognized that applications of GIS in large-scale projects demanded the investigations of social aspects of such applications of GIS and society inter-influence.

But more intriguing is another aspect of GIS in large social systems. That is we can say about increasing influences of GIS on the social processes, decision making, informational and PR technologies, education and management. Partially it is connected with the visualization of digital databases (tables, fails) in visual (cartographic) types.

The next key factor is the development of accesses to the personal computer. Moreover INTERNET and another networks support elaborated informational and communicational infrastructure. The interfaces of GIS have become more and more flexible and adjusted to the information consumer. We may anticipate that future interfaces in 'professional' GIS will be familiar with it in computer games.

And the third factor in GIS developing is that the society will became postindustrial with key role of informational technologies (IT). Thus the investigations of GIS influences will growth ([4] Klestova et al, 2001). The problems of optimal exploiting GIS of component IT also will be developed. Now such investigations (from the author's point of view) are at the initial stage. GIS roles will growth also in connections with distance education's, e-commerce, orientation systems as GPS, satellites communications and so on.

IT network in High Education. Themselves informational technologies networks are the transformation factors of high education. IT in such case became the direct social factor and their impact should be investigated and optimised on the strict methodological background including modelling.

Ethical aspects. Special attention should be paid to such a currently global aspect of ethics as interaction between science and international terrorism ([3] Klestova, Makarenko, 2002). Al-Qaeda showed an example of use of scientific achievements (aeroplanes, computers, satellite communication) for specific, alien to science (and to the society that had created them) purposes. Hence, an important question: is it acceptable to provide modern technologies to different type civilisations, especially bearing in mind the possibility of the notorious "struggle of civilisations", described by S. Huntington? It can be asserted that the civilisation boundaries are getting less physical and more internally built-in in the society due to globalisation and migration processes. It looks as if an opinion is being formulated in the scientific world in response to this vital question, that the solution should be thought not in terminating all contacts but in making contacts which will enable reduction of tension along the civilisations boundaries and in the growth of common interest areas. We would also like to place our expectations with the effectiveness of one of Warf's postulates, according to which language takes part in formation of consciousness. A common scientific language (and common goals) could become a relevant means of consciousness change in non-democratic countries. However, no rules can strictly regulate this process of a multiple interaction, and only personal ethical principles of the participants can ensure adequate control and self-restriction.

6. Ukraine case study

Ukraine description. Ukraine is sufficiently large country in Europe with large human potential (now about 46 millions habitats), large territory (607,7 thousand squire kilometer), and with still well developed educational system which had originated in USSR epoch. Currently many new students come to high education system every year. There is about 50 university of highest level in Ukraine. But unfortunately Ukraine has now only 10 billion dollars GNP each year, miserable mean salary (about 60 dollars per month, officially 341 hrivna per month in domestic currency at 1999 and about 250 dollars currently). All this follows to conflicts between high-level education system and industrial requirements, including informational technologies. Also one of the main sources of difficulties is command- administrative governance system which is analogs to it in former USSR. Particularly the useful information in education (including international) doesn't deliver to the working in educational process specialists. Also the old governance system suppresses the initiatives of basic (bottom level) educational units. Notwithstanding on such difficulties in Ukraine we still have a lot of educational units (departments, faculties, institutes and universities) with high level of education.

Negative trends. Some negative trends are common for all post- USSR countries. But Ukraine has specific problems. For example, Ukrainian education and scientific system is much less represented abroad. This restricts the possibilities for incorporating in international collaboration. Besides, Ukraine has less mineral resources than Russia and this follows to less level of mean salary. Next all recognise high level of corruption in Ukraine, which prevent from fast development. Also we have obsolete governance system and infrastructures. Nevertheless there exist some prospects for Ukraine in case of choosing some scenarios of development.

Possible place in Europe Almost independently on the development of domestic large industry Ukraine may take part in educational and scientific common space in Europe and in the world. Ukraine may prepare the young specialists for Western countries on the stable background. This will immediately improve the situation in Ukraine in the sphere of international relations and more important in transformations of Ukrainian society. Before the best carrier was through the governmental structures. The new role may open new possibilities and help to build civil society at Ukraine. Also Ukrainian researches may help to implement the scientific and technological investigations for developed countries. Of course for such goals it needs to have special infrastructures for education and technology transfers and scientific management (see [2] EWGTT, 2003).

Some propositions for cooperation in IT and HE. So such possible role of Ukraine forces the needs of further contacts and incorporating in international community. Many possibilities exist now from high governmental levels to the bottom level of individuals. In our fields of activities first of all it is involvement in different societies and non-formal activities. The second possibility is participation in different research and educational projects. Many possible issues and problems are represented implicitly in this report, especially at the next

166

section. And third is participating in exchange of students, lecturers, collaboration on strict background with universities and institutes.

7. Supplementary tools for supporting solutions

Mathematical modelling role. The role of mathematical modelling will increase, especially in concerned problems. The main source of modelling will be necessity in prognosing for such complex objects as large scales social systems, when the only personal experience of leaders can lead for wrong solutions with catastrophically consequences. This follows to development of models for social processes with accounting the behaviour and decision making in large collection of interacting individuals.

Decision support systems. The best examples of decision support systems now incorporate many different ideas from different fields - artificial intelligence, informatics, expert experience and many others. We suppose that in future DSS will incorporate more and more tools from classical automation including optimisation methods and also human factor containing modelling. Some of such models are described in ([6, 10] Makarenko, 1999, 2002; [5] Levkov, Makarenko, 1998).

GIS. The role of GIS as tool for saving, visualisation and preparing information will increase. Also GIS became society- transformation factor.

Technological foreseeing, forecasting, backcasting. Now developed countries try to make some investigations in such directions for the sake of future planning, anticipation and adaptation. Now Ukraine also makes some effort in this direction including scientific programs on such issues.

Social informatics. Till now the specialists on automations and control had deal mainly with mechanical or complex non-vital systems such as airplanes, space shuttles, power plants, factories, railway networks and so on. But recently all recognized that human factor and especially social psychology of large human systems would be one of the key problems. The global computerization and informatization gradually accelerate these processes of humanitarization. So in current conditions it is evident the necessity of creating and developing the tools for preparing the decision on the firm methodological background.

New educational specialty 'Social informatics' considers the problems of receiving, transformation, investigation, and modeling and explores the informational flows in large social systems and their models. Social informatics is complex interdisciplinary approach and consolidates the deep knowledge from mathematics and physics, computer sciences, management and humanity sciences ([8] Makarenko, 2001).

Gaming and Simulation. Gaming and simulation approach is one of the auxiliary tools for improving human organisations for large complex systems.

Non-governmental Organisations. It should stress possible role nongovernmental and non-formal organisations in preparing concepts of transformations and in dissemination the ideas and innovations through their networks. It is important that NGO as usually take a large part of activity at 'grass' level with individuals, target groups, elementary units. Important problem is optimisation of society - NGO interaction.

Mass- media. All recognise now the important role of mass- media. But here we would like to remember some aspects. Mass- media are very useful for dissemination information on educational and scientific issues. But it requires special investigations on the form of prepared information. Also mass- media influence is object of modelling.

Conclusion

Thus in proposed chapter we have tried to prepare a general outlook on the problems of IT, HE. We had considered as some general issues such as globalisation, international cooperation as particular problems, which concerned Ukraine. Also some research problems had been described in text of paper. The topics of paper may serve as background for further cooperation.

REFERENCES

1. EUROSCIENCE, (2003) (www.euroscience.org).

2. EWGTT, (2003) Euroscience Working Group on Technology Transfer. Ukrainian Branch (www.kiev.technology-transfer.net).

3. Klestova, Z., Makarenko , A. (2002) Conflicts of Interest between Eastern and Western Scientific Systems. *Ethics Science and Engineering Ethics*, Vol.**8**, No.3, pp. 387- 392.

4. Klestova Z., Makarenko A., Samorodov E. (2001) Geoinformational systems as technical tools for monitoring and decision- making in emergent situations and health care. *NATO ASI Series*. Kluwer AP, (Submitted).

5. Levkov S., Makarenko A. (1998) Geopolitical relations in post USSR Europe as a subject of mathematical modeling and control. *Preprints of SWIIS'98*, Sinaia, Romania, May, pp. 89-94.

6. Makarenko A. (1998) New Neuronet Models of Global Socio- Economical Processes. In *"Gaming /Simulation for Policy Development and Organisational Change"* (J.Geurts, C.Joldersma, E.Roelofs eds.), Tillburg Univ. Press, pp.133-138.

7. A. (1999) Anticipatory properties of participating of production systems and approach to their modelling. *Proc. ASI'99 Conf: Life cycle Approaches to Production Systems. Management, Control a*nd Makarenko *Supervision*, Leuven, Belgium, 6 pp.

8. Makarenko, A. (2001) Education and technology transfer in informational fields as the part of globalisation. In*"Lecture Notes in Informatics. Vol. **P-2**"*. (H.Mayr,), GI- Edition, Bonn, Germany.

9. Makarenko A. (2001) New technologies impacts on development of society. Environment, roles and actors. *Preprints of SWIIS'01*, Vienna, 2001.

10. Makarenko, A. (2002) Anticipating in modelling of large social systems - neuronets with internal structure and multivaluedness. *Int. J. Comput. Anticipation Systems*, Vol.**13**, 16 p.

11. Makarenko , A., Klestova, Z. (1999) A new class of global models of associative memory type as a tool for considering global environmental change. In *"Environmental. Change, Adaptation and Security"* (S.C.Lonergan, ed.), Kluwer, Pp.223-228.

www.ingramcontent.com/pod-product-compliance
Lightning Source LLC
Chambersburg PA
CBHW041220270326
41932CB00003B/11